Communicating for
Cultural Competence

COMMUNICATING FOR CULTURAL COMPETENCE

James W. Leigh
University of Washington

Allyn and Bacon
Boston • London • Toronto • Sydney • Tokyo • Singapore

Series Editor, Social Work and Family Therapy: Judy Fifer
Editor in Chief, Social Sciences: Karen Hanson
Editorial Assistant: Jennifer Muroff
Marketing Manager: Susan E. Brown
Production Administrator: Annette Joseph
Production Coordinator: Holly Crawford
Editorial-Production Service: Connie Leavitt, Bookwrights
Composition Buyer: Linda Cox
Manufacturing Buyer: Megan Cochran
Cover Administrator: Suzanne Harbison
Cover Designer: Jenny Hart

Library of Congress Cataloging-in-Publication Data
Leigh, James W.
    Communicating for cultural competence/James W. Leigh.
      p. cm.
    Includes bibliographical references (p.) and index.
    ISBN 0-205-18704-8
    1. Intercultural communication. 2. Communication in social work.
   3. Interviewing. I. Title.
    P94.6.L45   1997
    302.2—dc21   96-53189
                                           CIP

Printed in the United States of America
10 9 8 7 6 5 4 3 2   02 01 00 99 98

   Text credits: Page 18 from Yvonne S. Lincoln and Ergo Guba, *Naturalistic
Inquiry,* pp. 39–41, copyright © 1985 by Sage Publications, Inc. Reprinted by
permission of Sage Publications, Inc.
   Pages 25–28 from Richard W. Breslin, Kenneth Cushner, Craig Cherrie, and
Mahealani Young, *Intercultural Interactions: A Practical Guide,* pp. 267–301, copyright
© 1986 by Sage Publications, Inc. Reprinted by permission of Sage Publications, Inc.

  Text credits continue on page 189, which constitutes a continuation of the copyright page.

For My Parents, James and Pauline,
for Leading as Well as Following
and
Mary Jane, Ellen, Elmer, and Pauline

CONTENTS

PREFACE

Once during my early years as a social worker, I was working with a male adolescent African American who had problems with learning, problems in his relationships with both parents and peers, and trouble with acting-out behaviors. We were in an interview one day during the civil rights riots of the 1960s, and I was called out to respond to an emergency. When I returned, he had taken from my bookshelf a book on adolescent development. He read a passage to me and asked if these books were where I learned about him. My positive response led to a lesson I have not forgotten. "If you want to learn about me, you had better learn it from me." Learning from clients and having the client teach me, I must admit, was difficult. I had been educated to be the expert who assessed, diagnosed, and treated according to theories and research into the causes of human problems, and I knew what information I had to have to fulfill these professional functions. I entered into another phase of my education by learning to be a student of client teaching in the process of helping.

When I began my teaching at a school of social work, I attempted to convey my "practice wisdom" into practice courses. Encouraged by social work education's renewed interest with services to racially, culturally, and ethnically different populations in the 1970s, I began to reexamine the teaching of undergraduate and graduate students about issues involving the entry and retention of minority clients in the social services system. I began to deconstruct the practice that I had learned and to construct a practice that was more closely aligned with their lives. The multiethnic concentration of the school of social work began in 1974. Faculty, students, and guest lecturers began the process of the study of practice at the individual and family levels through the lens of race and culture. Surely we were influenced by the changes in society and the recognition that diversity and multiculturalism were dynamic and real factors in the delivery of social services in all fields of practice. The value of early concerns with racism in social work was openly incorporated into the teaching content. Along with this was the need for new ways of looking at social services to engage persons who essentially were looked on with fear, trepidation, and, sometimes, disinterest by the profession of social work. Out of this ferment developed a model for communicating with persons of color that cast them in the role of experts on their own lives.

The ethnographic interviewing procedures of James Spradley were adapted in 1982 for practice with people of color and first taught as part of the multiethnic practice concentration. Beginning in 1984, the interviewing model was taught as a separate course in the concentration. The model was taken outside the academic setting as a focus for workshops and presentations to agency in-service training sessions; professional organizational conferences such as the National Association of Black Social Workers, the Child Welfare League of America, Black Child Development Institute, the National Association of Social Workers, and the Council of Social Work Education.

The concepts and skills were introduced to faculty at other social work institutions of higher learning at Portland State University, Portland, Oregon; Wayne State University, Detroit, Michigan; Seattle University, Seattle, Washington; and Western State University, Kalamazoo, Michigan. In addition, the interviewing model became a part of curricula for the training of child welfare workers in Tennessee, California, and Michigan. These opportunities became field tests of the model. That it was well received resulted in its further development. The model is now being presented to a wider professional audience who have as their professional mandate the delivery of a social service to minority people of color.

I argue that the formation of a relationship is the base from which all professional and nonprofessional helpers must begin if they want to be successful in their cross-cultural helping endeavors. This can be done through the process steps outlined in this book. Work with individuals and families of color cannot ignore the way people of color are dealt with in the larger society. Professional social workers at the individual and family levels are change agents, and the change must begin with themselves.

The organization of this book is to make more specific the views in the preceding paragraphs. The first four chapters address information for achieving the role of the culturally competent social worker. The subsequent eight chapters outline the steps of the interview model based on the work of James Spradley as appropriate for social work practice. At the end of several chapters are exercises that have been used in my teaching to deepen the understanding of the chapter content. Others may develop exercises to fit their own course content and emphasis. Illustrations from interviews have been drawn from my practice, student practice, and published cases.

Emphasis is placed on the beginning stage of the helping process. This information-gathering stage is viewed as essential, and the model presented is front-loaded with specific steps to encourage the development of a positive relationship based on the client's role as a teacher of how his or her cultural world is viewed and why. What the social worker learns will become a framework within which problems are solved. If the beginning relationship is sound, the working and termination stages of help may proceed more efficiently and swiftly.

One may ask what is to occur after the ethnographic information is obtained? I have not addressed this issue directly in the major chapters of this book. In an effort to stimulate the reader's thinking, I have included Appendix C, which presents information on assessment, negotiated consensus treatment planning, and culturally relevant interventions and treatment. Specific process issues are to be addressed in future work. As all social workers must obtain information in order to arrive at an assessment and treatment plan, in this book I focus solely on the process of information gathering that lends itself to a culturally congruent assessment and treatment plan. If the information obtained is not relevant to the person of color, the assessment and treatment plan will not be viable in the work with people of color.

Entry into the world of the client to obtain the information is a recurrent theme. Once entry is accomplished, problem solutions will emerge based on the joint efforts of two people who are equal stakeholders in the process. I have identified the procedures of communication in the interview with persons of contrasting cultures in an effort to delineate a process that can be further researched and will strengthen cross-cultural practice with minorities of color.

ACKNOWLEDGMENTS

Many clients, friends, and students have had a profound influence on my teaching and development of the content of this book, which has been written to add another dimension to the delivery of effective and competent social services to people of contrasting cultures. I am particularly indebted to the students of the multiethnic practice concentration at the School of Social Work, University of Washington, who choose to study seriously practice with people of color and to gain cultural competency as a framework for this practice.

The transfer of the tasks of ethnographic interviewing from ethnography to social work practice with individuals and families was a joint effort with Dr. James W. Green of the Anthropology Department, University of Washington, who became my "cultural guide" into ethnography. Our early collaboration was intellectually stimulating and productive and indicative of the success of interdisciplinary endeavors. Our joint leadership of community and agency workshops furthered the testing of the material in a variety of social work settings with professional practitioners in child welfare, mental health, health, correctional, and child and family agencies.

No less appreciated is James R. Anderson, who provided a listening ear, supported and collaborated on many points of the work. His interest in learning and teaching the interviewing model and in negotiating the troubled waters encountered at the beginning of the multiethnic concentration demonstrated his professionalism, astute intelligence, and friendship. I am honored to have him as a friend.

I would be remiss not to recognize Dr. Calvin Takagi and Dr. Allethia Allen for their participation and leadership in the formation and development of the multiethnic concentration in 1974. The base for this book began with their personal experiences as people of color and their knowledge and concern for practice with people of color.

Nothing grows in a vacuum. The flowering garden is a result of the efforts of loving gardeners. The loving gardeners of my work have been my family, my friends, and the occasional stranger, all of whom listened as I told my story and believed in my progress. They encouraged a solo venture even when they knew not what the results would be. Their laying on of hands will always be gratefully remembered.

I am grateful to Allyn and Bacon who made this book possible, especially Judy Fifer, Series Editor; Karen Hanson, Editor in Chief; and Annette Joseph, Production Administrator, who all were patient, supportive, and encouraging guides. Finally, to the reviewers, I acknowledge my appreciation for their incisive comments and suggestions: Carmen I. Aponte, State University of New York, Brockport; Faith J. Bonecutter, University of Illinois, Chicago; Scott Burcham, Arkansas State University; and M. Jenise Comer, Central Missouri State University, Warrensburg.

1

INTRODUCTION

Every system that does not admit plurality
as the new way of life is exploding.
—*RYZSARD KAPUSCINSKI, 1988*

We can only speculate what the history of the United States would have been if the cross-cultural contacts in 1620 had resulted in an understanding of two worldviews based on an appreciation of the individual cultures. Steinberg (1981, 7) states that the Pilgrims, the settlers, "came not as immigrants entering an alien society, but as a vanguard of emigrants that would create a new England in the image of the one they left behind." The emigrants, as members of this vanguard referred to themselves, were persons fleeing from one country to another for economic, social, and political reasons. As they became the dominant cultural group, the emigrants began to guard against all outside encroachment on their culture. The manner of relating to the native population became the template for all future relationships with people who were not members of the emigrant culture. New immigrants were required to adapt to the dominant culture, language, and values. Persons of newly arrived status were oppressed by design, their cultures denigrated, and their languages viewed as inferior. They were asked to become American without benefit of equality and the social standing granted to Americans. This demand continues. In part it forms the basis for our contemporary concerns about people of contrasting cultures, whose worldviews conflict with those of the larger society and cause them to be viewed as problematic in economic, social, cultural, and political spheres of life.

The separatist stance of the major cultural group has affected the fabric of the society. Incorporation demands on the minority groups coupled with

1

regressive social policies have created severe problems for both dominant and minority populations. Cultural ethnocentrism prevailed and was exacerbated in the nineteenth century by racism based on skin color (Dubois, 1903; Murray, 1970; Berry & Tischler, 1978; Tumin & Plotch, 1977; See, 1986). Later aspects of racial thinking were transmitted to the public via pseudoscientific ventures that influenced and supported negative attitudes toward people of color beginning with African Americans (Szasz, 1971).

In the twentieth century, growth of ethnic minority populations in the United States occurred at a rapid pace (Cisneros, 1988; McAdoo, 1982). The complexion of the United States is changing. In 1995, Asians composed 3.3 percent of the population. In 2030, Asians will be 6.6 percent of the population; in 2050, Asians will be 8.2 percent of the population. Hispanics composed 10.2 percent of the population in 1995. In 2030, Hispanics will make up 18.9 percent of the population; by 2050, that figure will be 24.5 percent. In 1995, blacks composed 12.2 percent of the population. In 2030, blacks will compose 13.1 percent of the population; by 2050, that figure will be 13.6 percent of the population (*U.S. News and World Report*, 1996, 16).

Communities are struggling with the effects of these population changes on all facets of American life, particularly in the cultural area. What is essentially an American culture? Or is American culture a mixture of the cultures of the peoples of the country? For example, much discussion concerns the impact of African American music, poetry, and language on the cultural identity of the country (Ellison, 1964, 261–272; Murray, 1970; Bell, 1996, 146–148).

When contemporary problems of U.S. society are addressed, focus is on the newly arrived. *Time* magazine on July 8, 1985 stated, "They seem to come from everywhere, for all kinds of reasons, as indeed they always have" and "this enormous migration is rapidly and permanently changing the face of America. It is altering its racial makeup, its landscape and cityscapes, its taste in food and clothes and music, its entire perception of itself and its way of life" (26-27). Newly arrived groups historically have sought a place in the mainstream of society through assimilation, but many have not been able to accomplish this assimilation due to racism and the belittlement of their culture.

Minority cultural and racial groups of color attempt to adapt through a denial of their distinct racial and cultural heritage and through geographical migrations from one section of the country to another. These adaptations can only be viewed as responses to cultural ethnocentrism, prejudices, and institutional racism. Hine (1994) suggests that the migration of African American women grew not only from racial, social, and economic reasons but also from sexual exploitation intertwined with other oppressive actions that denied them control over their sexuality.

Population growth and racist practices place stress on all systems in the United States, including the social welfare system. This signals a new role for social workers as they become aware of how such changes affect the problems experienced by those of a contrasting culture, race, or ethnic group. The impact of ethnic minority growth is a recognized factor in the concern of social work to deliver viable social services not only to recent arrivals, but also to ethnic minority groups who have been in the United States for generations—for example, Native Americans and African Americans. Social work must respond in a manner different from that which social work history indicates. The issue of racism along with cultural relativism makes the problem more complex, more intransigent, and more demanding of solutions. Social work as a profession has not escaped the problems of providing services to persons who are victims of American separatist social practices and negative social policies. Berman-Rossi and Miller (1994) explored the settlement-house movement from the late nineteenth century to the 1930s. They point out that on the matter of race, early social workers conformed to the prevailing racism of society and reflected such thinking in their programs and policies:

> the preferred groups served by the settlements were European immigrants, not African American immigrants. Europeans were apparently thought to be better able to identify with and be influenced by cultural and social ideals of the settlements, their leadership and their "settlers." The goal of assimilation was apparently intended for European-Americans only. (33)

Since the Civil Rights movement of the 1960s, social work education has begun to address seriously the issues involved in practice as it affects America's racial, ethnic, and culturally contrasting populations (Dieppa, 1984; Gallegos & Harris, 1979; Chunn, Dunston & Ross-Seriff, 1983; Williams, 1988). There has been and continues to be an ebb and flow related to social work's concern with persons of contrasting racial, cultural, and ethnic identification in this century. Many questions have been raised through research and conceptual writing: Why should social work address the issue of cross-cultural practice in the United States? What is the intersection between culture and race as it impacts the process of helping? Is race the issue—or is it culture, class, or caste? What kind of professional social worker is needed to provide services to ethnic and culturally contrasting persons? What skills are needed, and what knowledge needs to be taught to prepare people to work effectively with minority persons and populations?

Such questions are recurrent and repetitive in the professional literature. The focus of this writing is to encourage the debate and to present a specific process skill that may be helpful for the social worker engaged in a helping relationship with persons who identify with a cultural background that is in distinct contrast to that of the social worker and the professional culture of social work.

This distinctiveness is often problematic for both the social work practitioner and the ethnic minority person. As all helping is offered within a specific cultural framework, must the person and the practitioner share the same framework if effective help is to be achieved? Is it essential that they hold the same values about family functioning and the roles of men and women in the family and culture? Do they agree on what helping is and how it is given?

The social worker and the person being helped both belong to and are part of an American multicultural society in which people embrace and cling to cultural patterns to retain a sense of identity and meaning. MacIntyre (1988) classifies both the dominant cultural group and the ethnic and minority groups as North American, but recognizes their lack of a common denominator with which to understand one another. Crucial to this cultural mix is the need to discover something in common between the two perspectives. Effective helping requires that the cultural gap be bridged. The people of North America come from a variety of cultural backgrounds and have a variety of stories to tell. In the professional helping endeavor, the client's storytelling needs to be encouraged as a beginning to filling the cultural gap between client and helper. Telling a story—a narrative—according to Young-Bruehl (1996, 466), provides "the need to master (if not overcome) the trauma, to make the world inhabitable again after it has been experienced as so malignant and so deadly." When the clients are minority persons of color, the encouragement of storytelling and belief in the stories can be therapeutic and a major benefit in the helping process.

A social worker should develop communication skills that elicit the ethnic minority person's narrative. It is in the narrative that the helper will find the client's hopes, aspirations, values, and views of the world. It is through the narrative that the client is understood, is helped, and feels better rather than through the theories about how people in distress improve, are helped, and are made to feel better.

Through telling and listening to stories, clients of diverse cultural groups and their social workers can engage in interactions whereby the service needs of both can be satisfactorily achieved. I believe that the profession of social work should focus on (1) how well the two parties in the helping encounter understand each other and (2) what methods the social worker can use to strive for this understanding. The key may lie in paying attention to the communication procedures through which the social worker may well develop an interactive skill that leads toward understanding a client who is culturally, racially, and ethnically different. This can happen as the story, the narrative, unfolds in the interview.

Issues that determine the formation of a positive relationship with clients have always been of concern to social workers. DeSchweintz (1948) instructed social workers to be courteous to clients. She taught courtesy as a means of showing respect for others. A simple example: not calling clients by their first names, a practice that is patronizing and authoritative. She promoted being civil as the underlying theme for social workers confronted with the poor, the destitute, the mentally ill, ethnic minorities, and others considered different from themselves. Social workers were urged to demonstrate civility through attitudes converted into behaviors. Civility involves problem solving in an atmosphere of respect as opposed to simply being nice, which camouflages differences and postpones hard decisions (Brewster, 1996, 23). On the basis of civility, the social worker tempers his or her attitudes to avoid letting ethnocentrism color what is heard and observed. The social worker views the person in a different, more positive light. The social worker is free to think about what the client is saying rather than about who the client is.

Fenalson (1962, 51) continued this early thrust by stating:

> The interviewer in human adjustment must be able to accept and understand individual differences in background, experiences, and attitudes as a basis for acceptance and understanding of the interviewee. The concept of culture contributes to such acceptance and understanding.

At the present time, a resurgence of emphasis on cultural factors is noted as social work continues to struggle with the idea of difference as it relates not only to ethnic minorities, but also to others representing difference from accepted, dominant cultural norms and values (Guberman, 1992). Arguments are strong regarding cultural factors related to the many populations of diversity. The social worker of the future may well have to be what is called the "culturally competent" social worker, possessing the important skill of eliciting the cultural narrative of the client. As our society grows more plural and equal, our social workers will be challenged to become effective cross-cultural interviewers.

Anthropologist Margaret Mead noted that her academic training taught her what to look for in the culture of others but not *how* to look for it (Mead, 1972, 151). How do you go about learning something about people who are culturally, ethnically, racially, and linguistically different from yourself? The how problem is not unfamiliar to social workers, who meet and work with persons whose ethnic, racial, and cultural groups contrast from their own. Social workers may know what to look for, but, like Margaret Mead, they worry about what procedures they should use.

I believe that such worries become diluted when the social worker engages the client in a dialogue, not a monologue. The dialogue is characterized by the telling of the narrative, through which the social worker discovers—in concert with the client—the route to effective problem solving.

A method for learning about others culturally is a recent development in ethnography. The procedures for ethnographic interviewing developed by James Spradley (1979) will be drawn upon as a tool for learning about the cultural imperatives of the ethnic minority person through the narrative. While learning how to do it, we must keep in mind why we are doing what we do. Social workers must view techniques and communication guidelines within a professional ethical and value framework and be governed by them in practice. Techniques of helping are constantly changing, and social workers must avoid the trap of using techniques and methods that do not fulfill the service needs of ethnic minority persons. Both social worker and client will lose. We must constantly consider the concepts of common human needs and the equality of individuals, as well as the value base of the social work profession. It is only through aligning concepts of acceptance, understanding, respect for human dignity, individuality, and community with our practice that social workers can explain the whys of helping skills with ethnic minority clients. Translating the concepts into the process of help is important.

Social work is committed to the creation of a society that holds promise and opportunity for all. Through our efforts as social workers, we attempt to "begin where the client is," and that means knowing where the client is culturally. Then the objective of assisting people to negotiate systems and find networks of support that are congruent with their lives and worldviews may well be met (Hollis & Wood, 1981).

We must engage in a process of learning from the ethnic minority person by listening to the narrative, the person's individual story. Through listening to another person's experiences, the social worker can learn what the other has already learned. Watson and Watson-Franke (1985) have termed this the "dialectical experience," an activity in which a former position is changed, new knowledge is obtained, and a new position is gained while a former position is lost or rejected. Both the person and the social worker can only gain in the process, as both are changed and their worldviews strengthened.

REFERENCES

Bell, Derrick. (1996). *Gospel choirs*. New York: Basic Books.

Berman-Rossi, Toby, & Miller, Irving. (1994). African Americans and the settlements during the late nineteenth and early twentieth centuries. *Social Work with Groups, 17*(3), 7–95.

Berry, Brewton, & Tischler, Henry L. (1978). *Race and ethnic relations* (4th ed.). Boston: Houghton Mifflin.

Brewster, David. (1996, March 20). The encumbered self. Quoting Betty Jane Carver. *Seattle Weekly*, pp. 17–23.

Chunn, Jay C., Dunston, Patricia J., & Ross-Sheriff, Fariyal (Eds.). (1983). *Mental health and people of color: Curriculum development and change*. Washington, DC: Howard University Press.

Cisneros, Henry. (1988). The demography of a dream. *New Perspectives Quarterly, 5*(2), 36–39.

deSchweintz, Elizabeth. (1948). *Courtesy: A requirement for the social worker*. Washington, DC: Federal Security Agency, Social Service Administration, Bureau of Public Assistance.

Dieppa, Ismael. (1984). Trends in social work education for minorities. In Barbara W. White (Ed.), *Color in a white society*. Silver Springs, MD: NASW.

Dubois, W. E. B. (1903). *The souls of black folk: Essays and sketches*. Chicago: McClurg.

Ellison, Ralph. (1964). *Shadow and act*. New York: Random House.

Fenalson, Ann. (1962). *Essentials in interviewing* (rev. ed. by Grace Beals Ferguson & Arthur Abrahamson). New York: Harper and Row.

Gallegos, Joseph, & Harris, Anita. (1979). Toward a model for the inclusion of ethnic minority content in doctoral social work education. *Journal of Education for Social Work, 15*(1), 29–35.

Guberman, Karen. (1992, Spring). Social work and the new diversity: How social work is responding to our changing society. *SSA Magazine*, p. 2.

Hine, Darlene Clark. (1994). Rape and the inner lives of black women in the middle west: Preliminary thoughts on the culture of dissemblance. In Ellen Carol Dubois & Vicki L. Ruiz (Eds.), *Unequal sisters: A multi-cultural reader in U.S. women's history* (pp. 292–297). New York: Routledge.

Hollis, Florence, & Wood, Mary. (1981). *Casework: A psychosocial therapy* (3rd ed.). New York: McGraw-Hill.

Kapuscinski, Ryzard. (1988). America as a collage. *New Perspectives Quarterly, 5*(2), 39–46.

MacIntyre, Alastair. (1988). *How to be a North American*. Washington, DC: Federation of State Humanities Councils.

McAdoo, Harriet. (1982). Demographic trends for people of color. *Social Work, 27*(1), 15–23.

Mead, Margaret. (1972). *Blackberry winter: My earlier years*. New York: William Morrow.

Murray, Albert. (1970). *The omni-Americans: New perspectives on black experience and American culture*. New York: Outerbridge and Dienstfrey.

See, Lethia A. (1986). *Tensions and tangles between Afro-Americans and southeast Asian refugees: A study of conflict.* Atlanta, GA: Wright.

Spradley, James P. (1979). *The ethnographic interview.* New York: Holt, Rinehart & Winston.

Steinberg, Stephen. (1981). *The ethnic myth: Race, ethnicity, and class in America.* New York: Atheneum.

Szasz, Thomas S. (1971). The sane slave. *American Journal of Psychotherapy, 25*(3), 226–239.

Time. (1985, July 8). Immigration: The changing face of America, 26–32.

Tumin, Melvin M., & Plotch, Walter. (1977). *Pluralism in a democratic society.* New York: Praeger.

U.S. News and World Report. (1996, March 25). Ahead: A very different nation, 16.

Watson, Lawrence C., & Watson-Franke, Maria-Barbara. (1985). *Interpreting life histories: An anthropological inquiry.* Brunswick, NJ: Rutgers University Press.

Williams, Leon F. (1988). Framework for introducing racial and ethnic content into the curriculum. In Carolyn Jacobs & Dorcas D. Bowles (Eds.). *Ethnicity and race: Critical concepts in social work* (pp. 167–184). Silver Springs, MD: NASW.

Young-Bruehl, Elisabeth. (1996). *The anatomy of prejudices.* Cambridge, MA: Harvard University Press.

2

BECOMING CULTURALLY COMPETENT

The best way to get inside yourself is to go
outside yourself, and as any good ethnographic
knows, if you cannot find yourself in the other,
you are not going to find yourself at all.
—RICHARD A. SHWEDER, 1986

Among the responses to advance social work practice with ethnic minorities and minorities of color, three models have been developed for practice with minority populations: *ethnic sensitive practice* (Devore & Schlesinger, 1981), *cultural awareness* (Green, 1982, 1995), and *social work process* (Lum, 1986). Each model endeavors to educate social workers as to what knowledge and attitudes are needed and what skills must be developed to engage in an effective practice. The framework for a culturally competent practice should be an anthropological–environmental focus supportive of the idea that cultures define solutions for problem-solving efforts (Krajewski-Jaime, Brown, Ziefert & Kaufman, 1996; Logan, 1985.).

Most models for practice with ethnic minorities of color have accepted the dual perspective notions of Norton, et al. (1978). The dual perspective refers to how people who identify with an ethnic minority interact with their own cultural group as well as with members of the larger society. Norton (1993) later raised questions about the dual perspective concept, which seemed to lead social workers to compare the two cultures. It is possible to recognize the two ambiguous and conflicting cultures, but "pushed to explain the lack of congruence between the two cultures one can arrive at an explanation of inherent deficit or blaming the victim" (Norton, 1993, 83). To view the minority culture negatively and the major culture as the one to be emulated would continue the negative evaluation of minority cultures.

An anthropological–ecological approach is more neutral in that it views human society as a set of control mechanisms that serve to meet the survival needs of the groups. Cultural patterns of various groups serve generic requirements. A cultural group can be explained and understood only through study of that group, not through study of the interactions between groups as the dual perspective suggests. This line of thinking implies that the social worker should learn the individual culture as it is lived by its members. The culturally competent social worker does not compare cultures pejoratively, but views them as "intricate, highly patterned systems of social inheritance through which each group of human beings attains and maintains the separate version of the humanity of its members" (Mead & Calas, 1953, xxii). Comparisons are to be avoided.

Cross-cultural practice begins, according to Lum (1986, 5), with the social worker discovering pertinent cultural information. The source of this information is the person being interviewed, who gives the social worker an insider's view of the culture rather than an outsider's view (Draguns, 1976, 2). Culturally competent social workers will respect these views and not impose their cultural interpretations on the information. To not do so would negate the expertise of others on aspects of their own lives. The culturally competent social worker functions effectively as a helper from the perspective of the cultural demands and worldviews of the minority person of color.

Green (1995, 89) defines the culturally competent social worker as one who "can provide professional services in a way that is congruent with behaviors and expectations that are normative for a given community." More specifically, competence in cross-cultural service requires a social worker who is aware of self-limitations, has a high interest in cultural contrasts, has a systematic learning style, can use cultural resources to help, and has basic knowledge about cultural groups (Dong, 1974; Miranda & Kitano, 1986). These characteristics are basic to the value system of a culturally competent social worker.

Cross, Bazron, Dennis, and Isaacs (1989, 22–24) present the following values for a culturally competent social worker:

1. Respect for unique culturally defined needs of various client populations.
2. Acknowledgment of culture as a predominant force in shaping behaviors, values, and institutions.
3. Belief that the family as defined by each culture is the primary and preferred point of intervention.

4. Acknowledgment that minority people are served in varying degrees by their natural cultural systems.
5. Recognition that the concepts of family, community, and so on differ among cultures and among subgroups within cultures.
6. Belief that diversity within cultures is as important as diversity between cultures.
7. Awareness that the dignity of the person is not guaranteed unless the dignity of his or her people is preserved.
8. Understanding that minority clients are usually best served by persons who are part of or in tune with their culture.
9. Acceptance that cultural differences exist and have an impact on service delivery.
10. Acknowledgment that process is as important as product when working with minority clients.
11. Awareness when values of minority groups are in conflict with dominant society values.

These values form the base for a culturally congruent approach to minority persons, families, and communities of color. They form a framework for the development of an information-gathering process that respects the cultural knowledge of the ethnic minority person and allows the social worker to obtain the insider's view and evaluation of the culture. The process of securing information that is congruent with this value set can be drawn from anthropology and ethnography (Green & Leigh, 1989). The goal of such technological transfer is the incorporation of a multicultural perspective in the delivery of social services, particularly when ethnic minorities are engaged in a helping process.

Social workers have contact with persons from a wide variety of racial, ethnic, cultural, and economic backgrounds. In spite of this, social workers are taught only a limited number of professional responses to variability. These responses are demonstrated first in skills and techniques used in the interview. They are the markers of the professional subculture.

Interviewing is the most consistently professional response in the delivery of human services. Effective human service delivery depends on effective communications. In cross-cultural helping situations, effective interviewing can be achieved through techniques and procedures that engage culturally contrasting individuals in a process that enables them to understand each other's perspectives.

It may be that a social worker's desire to help plus warmth and openness are not enough to engage ethnic minority persons in a process that takes into account their definitions and the meanings of their lives. Such concepts derive from a majority cultural set and may not be directly applicable to other cultures as the basis for relationship building. For example, the frequent comment "I understand" is meant to convey acceptance and empathy. But is this understanding based on an acceptance of the views of the minority person gained through the communication process with the minority person? When a social worker says "I understand," the motive is kindness, warmth, and generosity. However, understanding may exist between enemies or derive from knowledge of the power to injure through knowing another's weaknesses.

Communication, according to Thurman (1965), can occur only when the agendas of those in the communication process are the same. When each person's status is mutually accepted, communication occurs. A fellowship must be present; if not, contacts tend to express themselves in unsympathetic understanding without the healing spirit and energy of each person. With fellowship, suspicion is allayed, and intentionality pervades the communication process. Without fellowship, the communication process becomes an arena where each moves around in a world of shadows (Ellison, 1964, xxii).

The ethnographic model for interviewing is suggested for the culturally competent social worker because it fosters a fellowship with the minority person of color. This method of interviewing sets forth ways of gathering information in a nonthreatening manner. The procedures discourage the social worker from giving "meaning" to information and focus on learning about the other's cultural world through conversation.

Ethnographic interviewing is a method of inquiry in which the social worker controls the structure but not the content of the interview. Norton (1993, 89) states:

> Social workers' efforts to intervene on behalf of minorities need to be based on an understanding of the construction of meaning in the people's lives, not on external perceptions. It is a major challenge to ferret out these groups' worldviews and to create effective, responsible, valid policies and programs. . . . The search for meaning in another cultural context is complex.

The ethnographic model addresses this complexity by emphasizing that the expert on construction of meanings of any culture is a member of the culture, not a social worker. Key to its use is the social worker's acceptance of this premise. Ethnographic interviewing is a method of cultural discovery that requires the social worker to move beyond professionally bound methods of conversation with those who request assistance in solving personal or social-generated problems. The person being interviewed becomes the social worker's cultural guide, and this notion has an impact on the professional relationship. In some aspects the person is a teacher guiding the social worker as a student through the intricacies of the contrasting culture. The social worker has to become a skilled listener.

Attentive listening means more than simply hearing the person. It means that the person being interviewed is in some aspects the expert on defining the cultural implications and depth of the problem and that the opinions of this expert must be clearly understood before any analysis can begin (Mercer, 1996). In this model of interviewing, the ethnic minority person is the best possible teacher to assist the social worker in learning the culture of the other as part of the ethnosystem in which he or she resides.

The ethnosystem is a collection of interdependent ethnic groups sharing unique historical and/or cultural ties and bound together by a single political system (Solomon, 1976, 158). The ethnic minority person is a part of that ethnosystem as a member of the ethnic minority group. The task of the social worker is to discover the values, skills, and knowledge embedded in the person, the family, and the community. A discovery of the positive attributes of this single ethnosystem is the major task of the social worker in cross-cultural practice. This knowledge can prevent the social worker from looking at the contrasting culture from his or her own cultural perspective.

The culturally competent social worker, as a stranger, expects to be taught not randomly but through a set of skills that makes it possible to learn the views expressed in the cultural language. The set of technical skills was first suggested by Spradley (1979) to obtain a body of knowledge from the person in the culture. The techniques are contained within the ethnographic interviewing framework.

Ethnographic interviewing holds much promise for social workers who wish to attain cultural competence. Ethnographic interviewing can be very helpful when working with ethnic minority persons of color. Essentially, ethnographic interviewing is highly cognitive and word-oriented. It assumes that language and words, in particular, are windows to the world of the ethnic minority person. By ethnographic methods of inquiry, the social worker elicits the story. The story of a person can be seen as narrative through which the storyteller's perspective is revealed. Narrative is the universal metacode from which cultural messages and the nature of a shared reality are transmitted (Saari, 1991, 144; MacIntyre, 1988, 11). For effective helping, it is essential that the social worker hear the content of the narratives, as the content provides valuable information about how people experience others as well as themselves in interaction with others.

The culturally competent social worker encourages culturally contrasting people of color to tell their stories. The narrative is fact. Feelings and meanings about life situations result from remembrances of singular or group experiences. Andrews (1996, 214) speaks of the narrative process leading to reflection and the discovery of meaning. By having an opportunity to tell the story, the minority person begins a process of healing through self-discovery, self-definition, and movement away from the role of victim and subject. The stigma of being unable to sort out one's life experiences, identify their causes, and solve problems is mitigated in the process of narration. One form of narrative could be folktales that reflect perceptions of the contrasting culture's world, hopes, dreams, beliefs, customs, humor, frustrations, and problems as well as the means for solving problems. Greenbaum and Holmes (1983) urge the eliciting of folktales to assist in establishing rapport and as a possible avenue toward problem solving.

Narratives are delivered through spoken and written words. The culturally competent social worker must deal with the issue of language as a component of the helping process. Words make up the totality of narrative. Words label; they impose an order on perception; they create categories of things and their worth. In some instances, words are weapons. Words can mystify, they can be threatening, and they can be offensive (Moore, 1992). The language the social worker uses in the interview can serve as a detriment and barrier to understanding. The culturally competent social worker is aware that professional language can serve as a hindrance to the helping process.

The feelings of separateness experienced by many ethnic minority persons in helping situations can be the result of a social worker's insensitivity to the person's cultural language uses. Social workers may use professional jargon to protect their status and maintain authority over people seeking their help. This language is a product of their acculturation to the profession of social work. Only other social workers understand it. When used in the professional encounter, it creates a sense of alienation and separateness on the part of the ethnic minority person. If social workers view themselves as part of—and reflecting—the professional culture and language, they may be unable to control the use of professional language and attend to their understanding of the cultural language of the ethnic minority person.

Social work's efforts to develop an understanding of the ethnic minority person must begin with efforts to understand the uses and abuses of its own professional language and what language may stand for in the culture of the minority person. Words not only open the world of the other; they can also conceal the world of the other. In a culture that values civility, even though everyone does not love or respect everyone else, respect is possible through the language of civility. Respect for one another occurs not only through civil discourse but also through activities which reduce isolation. The formation of positive relationships creates a community where two or more people achieve a sense of common purpose.

Language variations—even within a linguistic group such as English—are the most significant markers of ethnic and cultural diversity. Language has a social function in that through it individuals express something of their origins, personal values, and social status in relation to others inside and outside the group. Language relates to thought processes, and because languages vary within any one cultural group, it follows that speakers of different languages will perceive and therefore construct reality differently. To learn the use of another's language is to enter into the world of the other. That should be the goal of all social workers in cross-cultural work.

A social worker can become culturally competent by gaining the skill of communicating competently with people of contrasting cultures. To rely on empathy alone is not enough. The social worker must strive for the degree of understanding that can derive only from information provided by a member of the contrasting cultural group. Failure to achieve this means the social worker cannot enter into the senses of the other. The social worker must comprehend the cultural context and meaning of these sensibilities. Only then will the social worker comprehend what it is that the person knows and how that knowledge is used in everyday life. Once meaning is revealed, meaning is known, and caring follows.

REFERENCES

Andrews, William L. (1996). *The Oxford Frederick Douglass reader*. New York: Oxford University Press.

Cross, Terry L., Bazron, Barbara J., Dennis, Karl W., & Isaacs, Mareasa R. (1989). *The cultural competence continuum: Towards a culturally competent system of care*. Washington, DC: Georgetown University Child Development Center.

Devore, Wynetta, & Schlesinger, Elfriede. (1981). *Ethnic sensitive social work practice*. St. Louis: C. V. Mosby.

Dong, Clarene N. (1974). Clinical social work practice. In F.L. Feldman (Ed.), *Social work papers* (pp. 48–59). Los Angeles: University of Southern California.

Draguns, Juris G. (1976). Counseling across cultures: Common themes and distinct approaches. In Paul Pedersen, William J. Lonner, & Juris G. Draguns (Eds.), *Counseling across cultures*. Honolulu, HI: The University of Hawaii Press.

Ellison, Ralph. (1953). *Shadow and act*. New York: Random House.

Green, James W. (1995). *Cultural awareness in the human services* (2nd ed.). Boston: Allyn & Bacon.

Green, James W., & Leigh, James W. (1989). Teaching ethnographic methods to social service workers. *Practicing Anthropology*, *11*(3), 8–10.

Greenbaum, Lenora, & Holmes, Ivory H. (1983). The use of folktales in social work practice. *Social Casework*, *54*(7), 414–418.

Krajewski-Jaime, Elvia R., Brown, Kaaran Strauch, Ziefert, Marjorie, & Kaufman, Elizabeth. (1996). Utilizing international clinical practice to build inter-cultural sensitivity in social work students. *Journal of Multicultural Social Work*, *4*(2), 15–29.

Logan, Sadye. (1985). Review of *Color in a white society*. *Social Work*, *30*(4), 376.

Lum, Doman. (1986). *Social work practice and people of color*. Monterey, CA: Brooks/Cole.

MacIntyre, Alastair. (1988). *How to be a North American*. Washington, DC: Federation of State Humanities Councils.

Mead, Margaret, & Calas, Nicolas. (1953). *Primitive heritage*. New York: Random House.

Mercer, Susan. (1996). Navajo elderly people in a reservation nursing home: Admission predictors and culture care practices. *Social Work, 41*(2), 181–189.

Miranda, Manuel R., & Kitano, Harry H. L. (Eds.). (1986). *Mental health research and practice in minority communities: Development of culturally sensitive training programs*. Rockville, MD: National Institute of Mental Health.

Moore, Robert B. (1992). Racist stereotyping in the English language. In Margaret L. Anderson & Patricia Hill Collins (Eds.), *Race, class, and gender* (pp. 317–329). Belmont, CA: Wadsworth.

Norton, Dolores G. (1993). Diversity, early socialization, and temporal development: The dual perspective revisited. *Social Work, 38*(1), 82–90.

Norton, D. G., with Brown, E. F., Brown, E. G., Francis, E. A., Mirase, K., & Valle, R. (1978). *The dual perspective: Inclusion of ethnic minority content in social work education*. New York: Council on Social Work Education.

Saari, Carolyn. (1991). *The creation of meaning in social work*. New York: Guilford Press.

Shweder, Richard A. (1986, September 21). Storytelling among the anthropologists. *New York Times Book Review, 7*(1), 38–39.

Solomon, Barbara B. (1976). *Black empowerment: Social work in oppressed communities*. New York: Columbia University Press.

Spradley, J. (1979). *The Ethnographic Interview*. New York: Holt, Rinehart and Winston.

Thurman, Howard. (1965). *The luminous darkness*. New York: Harper and Row.

3

NATURALISTIC INQUIRY
A Base for Cultural Competence

The key to the presumed generality can only be
found in the merciless particular.
—*JAMES BALDWIN, 1985*

Ethnographic interviewing has a theoretical base in naturalism, and the procedures follow guidelines presented in naturalism. According to Hammersley (1990, 7), naturalism aims to capture the character of naturally occurring human behavior, which can be achieved only through first-hand contact, not through inferences derived from outside the culture.

Inductive rather than deductive thinking is the thrust of naturalism. The naturalist process of discovery uses minimal hypothesis to maximize one's capacity for learning. The ethnographic approach to interviewing, rooted in naturalism, has as a starting point general interest, which makes the discovery process a narrowing process sharpened and changed as it proceeds based on what is learned (Hammersley, 1990, 8).

Ethnographic interviewing may be of assistance to social workers who desire to learn about the cultural imperatives of clients whose cultures contrast with their own. Social workers who adopt an educational stance have to be able to hear new information without feeling that their self-esteem is being assaulted, their ego is being assaulted, or their own sense of cultural identity is being undermined.

An understanding of naturalism and naturalistic inquiry helps the social worker understand the purpose of ethnographic interviewing. Lincoln and Guba (1985) cite several precepts in a naturalistic paradigm that are connected to the belief system of the person. While belief systems cannot be proven, they can be seen operating in the behavior of people. As the person thinks, so the person acts.

Paradigms are models or patterns. They define boundaries that restrict thinking and behavior. Paradigms are also enabling in that they form a framework for behavior and possible actions. The reason for action or behavior lies hidden in the paradigm and its unquestioned assumptions. Therefore one may view the behavior of another but fail to understand it. Social workers cannot know the "why" of behavior unless they are privy to the assumptions of its paradigm.

The process of helping begins with an attempt to discover "where the client is." The social worker embarks on a process of social research with the case as the focus of the information gathering. From the gathered information, the social worker formulates an hypothesis about the present situation in order to design an intervention plan that will affect the future. Here guidelines from the naturalist framework may be helpful (Denzin, 1971).

According to Lincoln and Guba, the characteristics of naturalistic inquiry are as follows:

1. In natural setting considerations, realities of the person cannot be separated from their contents, nor can they be separated out for the study of the parts. The whole is more than the parts.
2. The person is the data gathering instrument because of the adaptability needed to encompass and adjust to the varieties of reality that will be encountered.
3. A use of tacit knowledge is valid. Intuition and feelings are as valid as knowledge expressed in language because most of the interactions between two people occur this way and because tacit knowledge mirrors patterns of the investigators.
4. Negotiated outcomes are important. Negotiated meanings and interpretations between inquirer and the person are necessary because it is the latter's construction of reality which the former wishes to reconstruct.
5. Findings are considered tentative. The naturalistic inquiry results in a hesitation to make broad generalizations because realities are multiple and different and because findings are dependent on interactions between investigators and respondents and may not be duplicated because of the values, settings, experiences, and the particular persons involved (Lincoln & Guba, 1985, pp. 39–41).

If the social worker follows the naturalistic inquiry guidelines, the intervention will grow out of the interaction between the social worker and the person interviewed. The plan is emergent, not preordained, because what is learned by the social worker has a base in the personal interactions. Thus the action results are unpredictable. The problem-solving interventions must result from the interactive process that unfolds. Social workers who use the naturalistic model and ethnographic techniques of information gathering begin a case situation not knowing what they do not know (Lincoln & Guba, 1985, 4), whereas traditional information-gathering guidelines imply that social workers know what they do not know.

To not know what you do not know does not mean that you know nothing. Tacit knowledge may provide a connection with the presenting problem or presented person. Tacit knowledge is knowledge understood but not stated. You may have intuitions and feelings as a result of earlier information-gathering efforts such as formal learning or previous work experiences. Recognizing this, the social worker practicing naturalistic inquiry is cautious about transferring what has been learned from one person to the case of another person. As the contacts continue, salient features of the client's worldview emerge; insights develop, and a theory grounded in analysis of the new information takes shape.

An essential component in the naturalistic inquiry model of information gathering is the establishment of trust. As the paradigm demands, the establishment of trust is not merely a matter of applying information-gathering techniques and being nice to the person. Trust requires more than simple empathy, warmth, and acceptance.

The criteria for trust must be fully and adequately met. A major factor in trust is credibility in the eyes of the applicant for service (Lincoln & Guba, 1985, 213). According to Sue and Zane (1987), credibility in the helping process occurs when the applicant for service views the social worker as a "gift giver." Giving gifts is not unusual in the beginning stages of cross-cultural encounters, as many cultural groups exchange food, small items of cultural relevance, and hospitality as a means of establishing acceptance. Historical narratives are noted for the gift giving, and these narratives are depicted in the graphic arts of cultural meetings focused around exchange of articles such as beads, pelts, foods, and clothing. The genuine offering of self as a helper can be a gift of the social worker.

Trust is a developmental process engaged in whenever the social worker is in the context of the other person. Within the professional helping situation, the social worker is actually within the context of another life. The social worker has to demonstrate certain things: that confidences will not be used against the person; that what the person reports will be validated; that attempts will be made to learn; that the person has the strength to teach, to explain, and to describe his or her social cultural situation. Trust is instilled when the person has input into and actually influences the inquiry process in some matter. If trust is destroyed, and it can be, it takes a long time to mend.

Sometimes broken trust is not repairable. Lack of trust in the social worker often causes ethnic minority individuals to discontinue the helping process. The following case is illustrative.

Case Illustration

A social worker noted that very few Native Americans were using the agency services. Agency statistics revealed that Native American clients were retained at a lower rate than any other client group. The social worker had little direct experience working with Native American clients, and those that had been assigned to her did not keep appointments or did not return after one interview. No one in the agency had formally questioned the issue. Informal conversations with other agency workers revealed that they thought the Native American was a poor client, difficult to talk to, and in need of services more concrete than agency counseling.

The social worker had an opportunity to attend an in-service training session where ethnographic interviewing was taught. She decided to try the ethnographic interview model and asked the next Native American assigned to her to be her cultural guide.

As the social worker began using the ethnographic model for interviewing, her main action was active listening, with the objective of learning about the cultural context of the Native American applicant. The social worker focused her global questions in the area of the cultural context of mental illness, problem solutions, and roles of the helpers within the cultural context of the applicant's life. The applicant agreed to assume the role of cultural guide or informant only after a brief hesitation as to her ability to explain the cultural context of the problems she was experiencing.

As the ethnographic data and information unfolded in the interviews, the social worker learned much about the "wound in the spirit" and discovered the importance of dreams in the applicant's culture. This learning was checked back with the applicant for correction and interpretation. The collaborative effort at understanding the meaning of the cultural imperatives resulted in an intervention plan to aid in the solution of the presenting problem. Treatment strategies focused around dreams and associated situations that had important cultural meaning to the applicant, who became a client and continued with contacts for fourteen months and reported significant progress in the solving of the presenting problems. The case was closed as successful.

The social worker in our example was concerned with the successful treatment of Native Americans and was willing to suspend traditional methods of information gathering to increase her success rate. She began with a case research focus and adopted a naturalist paradigm to further her understanding of the person. She relied on a fundamental technique, namely that understanding meant "the process by which the practitioner seeks to totally apprehend human beings, their inner minds, and their feelings, and the way these are expressed in their outward actions and achievements" (Rodwell, 1987, 232). Naturalism does offer a method for obtaining richer assessment data than do the usual methods based on medical and deterministic models.

The emphasis in social work on finding out the right answers through scientific or empirical approaches can be questioned (Rodwell, 1987). Although strongly advocating for attention to the persons' perceptions of their reality, Rodwell does not explicate the process of interviewing that a social worker might use to discover the cultural world of the ethnic cultural person. The focus for Rodwell is on the assessment of the process in which the social worker becomes an investigator who ferrets out the other's intentions, thoughts, feelings, and actions while being sensitive to the multiple realities of family members. The information obtained will be necessary for assessment and treatment planning.

The naturalistic paradigm is the working base for social work practice derived from values of the uniqueness of the individual and the interdependence of people in shaping the potential of each. The social worker may well be supporting the basic values of social work by using the naturalistic model and ethnographic interviewing. Rodwell (1987, 243) supports this view, asserting: "The naturalistic paradigm provides different assumptions, different expectations, and supports the profession [of social work] value based behaviors. It allows the exploiting of opportunities that interaction with clients affords. It becomes not only acceptable but desirable to have a close, meaningful relationship with a client. . . . The inquiry procedures that ask for ideographic interpretations and negotiated outcomes and that allow the worker to recognize and to act on tacit knowledge result in an assessment that proceeds meaningfully and that produces findings and interpretations agreeable from all perspectives."

EXERCISE

The following exercise will aid in your understanding of credibility and giving.

The Case of Mr. Alcott

After a second admission to the hospital, John Alcott was referred to the mental health clinic by his doctor for assistance with family matters.

A review of the hospital record revealed that Mr. Alcott was African American, 27 years old, and had been admitted several times for alcoholism. The medical staff recorded that he would not follow medical advice. According to his doctor, Mr. Alcott agreed to attend the mental health clinic only because of his three-year-old child.

In addition to his drinking, Mr. Alcott reports that his friends describe him as crazy when he tells them he hears voices. At times he thinks he loses control when he drinks and assaults his wife. His wife comes to visit him in the hospital but remains only for a short time. Usually an argument ensues and she leaves. Once the nurses asked her to leave because of the arguing. It was after this incident that the referral was made to the mental health clinic.

Mr. Alcott is being released from the hospital within the next three days. He accepted the referral from his doctor reluctantly and does not understand how a social worker can help him. He does want to be home with his daughter.

Directions

You are the social worker assigned to Mr. Alcott. You have recently read about the concepts of credibility and gifts as outlined in the reading by Sue and Zane (1987).

Using the concepts, answer the following questions.

1. What would be my level of credibility with Mr. Alcott?
2. How could I enhance my credibility with Mr. Alcott?
3. What gifts shall I provide during the initial phase of the helping process?
4. How can I evaluate the effectiveness of credibility and gift giving?

REFERENCES

Baldwin, James. (1985). *The evidence of things not seen.* New York: Holt, Rinehart & Winston.

Denzin, Norman K. (1971). The logic of naturalistic inquiry. *Social Forces, 50*(2), 166–182.

Hammersley, Martyn. (1990). *Ethnographic research: A critical guide.* New York: Longman.

Lincoln, Yvonna S., & Guba, Ergon G. (1985). *Naturalistic inquiry.* Beverly Hills, CA: Sage.

Rodwell, Mary K. (1987). Naturalistic inquiry: An alternative model for social assessment. *Social Service Review, 61*(2), 231–246.

Sue, Stanley, & Zane, Nolan. (1987). The role of culture and cultural techniques in psychotherapy: A critique and reformation. *American Psychologist, 42*(1), 37–45.

4

KNOWLEDGE

The Foundation for Cultural Competence

I will learn to listen to the wisdom of the blues.
—ROBERT FLEMING, 1996

Harold Lewis (1982) is correct when he urges social workers to operate as master professionals on the basis of knowledge. To engage in a social service practice that is informed by research, theory, and concepts should be the goal of every social worker. Complete knowledge about the human condition is impossible to attain, as the body of information is continually changing and developing. Nevertheless, social workers can have an informed practice based on knowledge, not intuition, if they develop a stance that permits them to learn as they practice. Understanding of self as a helper and person should be seriously considered in forming a knowledge base for cross-cultural social work practice. Problems with persons of another culture may be attributable to a social worker's personal attitudes that create barriers to effective cross-cultural practice. By self-examination and introspection, social workers can deepen their professional capabilities and maintain a humble stance in the face of changing client populations and changing views of what causes social ills and problems.

SEEKING CONCEPTUAL KNOWLEDGE

To become proficient in cross-cultural practice, the social worker should utilize resources that offer helpful information. Gil (1984, 20–21) asserts:

A basic principle in working with ethnic persons is that the workers have an obligation to seek knowledge about the person's culture in order to better understand ethnically related responses to illness. This can be done by reviewing relevant anthropological and sociological literature, talking with staff who are familiar with the person's culture, through discussion with other members of the same ethnic group, or by simply asking the person to tell his/her own cultural story.

Learning from the ethnic minority person of color is a prime area for learning in relation to ethnographic interviewing and will be addressed in other major sections of this book. Learning about ethnic, cultural, and racial groups from the relevant anthropological and sociological literature is important, as this learning may be the first exposure the social worker has to ethnic minority populations of color. Whatever is learned in the course of formal studies may have an important impact on the social worker's service delivery to persons of color. Therefore emphasis will be placed here on learning through formal educational channels.

Opportunities to learn about ethnic minorities of color in formal educational settings are not even throughout the social work education system. Critics of services given to ethnic minority persons of color often cite the lack of planned educational approaches and curriculum to prepare social workers to deal with the issues that arise in helping relationships with persons whose ethnic, cultural, and racial backgrounds differ from their own. This lack of focus on cultural content and its impact on human development and problems experienced in everyday life by ethnic minority persons of color is frequently mentioned as a major reason for the difficulties minorities encounter in the social welfare system. The literature does suggest areas of learning about ethnic minority populations, and these areas will be presented in this section as a guide for further learning.

Many other professions face similar educational issues in preparing students for cross-cultural practice. Kleinman (1988b), for example, urges psychiatry to include content on culture in the educational curriculum of psychiatrists. For the beginning trainee, Kleinman suggests a focus on cultural values, behavioral norms and practices, cultural styles of communication, and family and other social institutions that can influence behavior. As the trainee moves through the educational process, ethnographic material on illness and illness-related behaviors as well as methods of helping and healing might be added. Other suggested areas of study include child development cross culturally, child abuse in particular cultural contexts, adolescent issues related to cultural demands, and school and drug abuse in different cultural settings.

The education of every social worker should include material related to the varieties of ethnic minority persons of color in the ethnosystem of the United States. The student of any helping profession, including social work, should be required to complete courses that address the issues of culture and its relevance to ethnic minority populations. Cross et al. (1989) express the opinion that social work has yet to define what should be known by the social worker for practice with ethnic minority populations of color. Progress has been noted in that material on cultural groups has been more prevalent than in past years, but material on culture and its impact on human behavior has been given less emphasis.

The social worker's knowledge prior to initial contact is important because the ethnic minority person may expect the social worker to know something about the culture to which he or she relates. If social workers have not developed an understanding of cultural differences as reflected in daily living tasks, they will experience cultural shock when confronted with a person who communicates and behaves differently from their expectations. Social workers are asked to enter into another culture when working with ethnic minority persons of color. Breslin, Cushner, Cherrie, and Young (1986) suggest the following areas for culture-related study.

Work

Entering a new work place can be culturally upsetting. One characteristic of the work place is that it is a common ground for many people of contrasting cultures to come together. A person does not have control over the selection of individuals with whom one must work. In some work situations those who decide on who should be employed may choose on the basis of cultural sameness rather than cultural contrasts.

In the cross-cultural situation, individuals bring with them particular ways of interacting and particular expectations of others that may be different from the behaviors and beliefs of others in the organization. This may be the basis for much discomfort on the part of culturally identified persons who do not share a similar cultural framework with other organizational workers. This may be compounded when the consumer group is identified culturally with a worker and the other workers are believed to be insensitive, unhelpful or disinterested in helping the consumer group.

Time

Time perspectives have a distinct cultural reference and can be one of the most distressing features of cross-cultural interactions. If one person is bound by a Euro-American time frame and interacts with a Native American operating on time as related to environmental changes, problems can occur. To avoid these problems, the social worker needs to understand time references from the other's point of view. The social worker might also check with experienced persons from their own culture or someone from the other culture for exact time reference.

Space

When we interact with others in a given space, cultural imperatives are guiding forces. A violation of one's cultural demand for territory and space is the most common cross-cultural error. Distance between bodies identified with a given culture remains constant. Some cultures keep short distances between bodies; others, longer distance. Space between individuals is a culturally determined and maintained practice. Physical touching, closeness, distance, eye contact are all space issues.

Language

In crossing language barriers, one finds words, phrases or concepts not found in one's own language. Even similar words in two cultures have different meanings. This is particularly true of slang and colloquialisms. Language is a reflection of culture. Words are used to transmit culture. The social worker needs to be sensitive to words and their meanings to others of a different culture. The social worker ought to assume a learning stance towards language and be prepared through knowledge for the possible meanings of popular phrases and words of the culture. One's attitude towards another culture can be readily demonstrated in how one approaches the language issue.

Roles

The range of roles that people occupy have a base in culture. Family roles can be differentially distributed. The role of mother, father, child may be totally different between cultural groups. Family may be nuclear, extended, matriarchal, patriarchal or determined by blood lineage. Sex roles are culturally determined. Male-female interactions may differ between groups. A knowledge of roles is essential in cross-cultural encounters.

Group/Individualism

The degree of individualism versus collective behaviors differs between cultures. The extent to which an individual submits self to collective demands can be wide. Most persons are not aware of this cultural imperative. Group decisions can override individual demands, wishes or desires. Issues effecting one's life can be subject to group decisions, not individual decisions.

Ritual and Superstition

Rituals pervade aspects of society to varying degrees and may exist both as commonly agreed upon societal forms and as more idiosyncratic individual forms. Rituals serve as social communications (hand shaking, bowing, etc.), to provoke power (calling upon a supernatural being), or as a statement of belief (gospel singing). Rituals are based on symbolic concepts. They represent relationships of kinship, or participation in and connection with physical, organic, psychological realities of society. Rituals can be viewed as body actions or participation in relation to symbols.

Superstition generally carries more pejorative connotations than rituals. The acts are viewed as having no base in reality but can be powerful forces to those who hold them. The social worker in cross-cultural encounters should be cautious in assigning an irrational label to particular acts or beliefs and learn how they may operate in a given culture. This prepares the social worker to accept their value to the other.

Class and Status

Whenever two people get together, a hierarchy develops and certain norms operate as to who is the leader, who is the follower and who gives direction. Those at the top exert more power in the interaction. Power seems to be an integral part of class and status. Power is the ability to control the behavior of others. A powerful person differs from an influential person in that other people perceive more choices about behaving when the latter type of person makes a suggestion.

Class may be related to family, occupation, residence, economic status or value structures. It can be an operating variable in discriminatory activity; it can be a motivating factor for social mobility.

In cross-cultural encounters, the person may view the social worker from his or her own cultural perspective as being a person of high status with power. The social worker's imperative may be the opposite. Knowledge of the variety of ways cultures look on power and influence is an important knowledge area.

Values

Values are weights with which people evaluate or judge their world. People make judgments and come to a conclusion about what is and what is not of value. These values are learned as a part of a person's socialization to a culture. Values reflect a culture's view towards central issues of politics, economics, religion, aesthetics, personal relationships, morality and the environment. Cultural differences and conflicts arise from the fact that individuals and societies order these values in different hierarchies. (Breslin, Cushner, Cherrie, & Young, 1986, pp. 267–301)

Problems can arise when the social worker attempts to function in his or her own value system while at the same time wanting to identify with another value system. This needs to be addressed in learning about other cultures. Through such knowledge the social worker may develop a flexibility which will allow an easy adaptation to fresh and different perspectives on the issues of values.

Wilson (1982) delineates additional knowledge areas for social workers striving to become culturally competent when working with minority groups of color:

1. Knowledge of the culture (history, traditions, values, family systems, and artistic expressions).
2. Knowledge of the impact of class and ethnicity on behavior, attitudes, and values.
3. Knowledge of the help-seeking behaviors of ethnic minority clients.
4. Knowledge of the role of language, speech patterns, and communication styles in ethnically distinct communities.
5. Knowledge of the impact of social services on ethnic minority persons.
6. Knowledge of resources (agencies, persons, informal helping networks, research) that can be utilized on behalf of ethnic minority clients and communities.
7. Knowledge of the ways that professional values may conflict with or accommodate the needs of ethnic minority clients.
8. Knowledge of the power relationships in a community, agency, or institutions and their impact on ethnic minority clients.

These areas that social workers may explore in their learning quest encompass the totality of worldviews of ethnic minority persons. English (1984) writes that worldviews are defined as a class of concepts that define ways people perceive relationships to nature, institutions, other people, and objects.

A review of the literature related to ethnic minority populations reveals that the knowledge base generally falls into two distinct areas. The first is knowledge about specific ethnic minority groups such as African Americans. In this area the social worker would, for example, learn about specific historical events that have impinged and impacted the African American group's present social/psychological state. In addition, the social worker would learn about family structures and group concepts of time and roles of group members in relationship to one another.

The second general area is knowledge that explicates central concepts necessary to understanding the ethnic minority position in society and how those concepts function on the development of human behavior. The social worker studying in this area would concentrate on learning about race, racism, stereotyping, ethnicity, culture, integration and separatism, and biculturalism.

Social workers in a child welfare agency engaged with ethnic minority persons were asked to suggest areas of knowledge they thought would be most important in their work with their clients. The majority identified the range of culturally acceptable child-rearing behaviors within an ethnic minority group as most important (Talbert & Sullivan, 1988). Others were knowledge of rituals and rites and behaviors in these areas; knowledge of differences between various cultures; and knowledge about the acceptable roles and attitudes of social workers within ethnic minority groups.

There is a wide range of literature that social workers can tap as they strive to learn about ethnic minority populations. This section has suggested some of the major areas to be studied. Once one has learned about ethnic minority populations from formal educational resources, how learning is used in the process of help becomes crucial. These knowledge areas will assist the social worker to become more informed about the ethnic minority person. But there is a danger of using the material not to become more understanding but to view the minority group as lesser in value than one's own group. Social workers must continually examine themselves as to the impact of learning on their own perceptions of others. They must be aware of personal attitudes that stereotype the minority individual and group.

CENTRAL TENDENCIES

Central tendency material is gained from generalized knowledge. Generalized knowledge can be defined as group cultural factors. Axelson (1985, 34) states that generalized knowledge is "the background of a group of people." As a result of historical experiences, a group devises and selects worldviews that come to be known as traditional over the years. These worldviews consist of thoughts, behaviors, accepted roles, designated manners of handling daily activities, and values. The most obvious aspects of a group's culture are the ideas, beliefs, and values that worldviews are based on. Developing over time, the group's cultural behaviors, thoughts, and activities show a pattern of preference for the ways of the group as it interacts with the larger world. People within the culture show a preference for a mode of action even when other paths are open to them.

It is important for the social worker in a multicultural system to understand this preference for a mode of action. People coming for assistance will act in the helping situation consistently with the demands of their own cultural imperatives. If the social worker has learned to be aware of the central tendencies of a given culture, then differentiation can be made between groups. Nevertheless, the social worker should be cautious about the applicability of this material to the individual within the group.

The social worker must be flexible in the use of language that is culture bound and engage in efforts with the person to discover how that person's action mode compares to the cultural imperatives of the group with which the person identifies. Learning central tendencies of a group can lead to a very structured, logical approach to a person, but also may serve to stereotype the person.

Culture is a problem-solving device and a technical tool that facilitates the helping process and should not be viewed as an impediment to it. The core of any group's culture is "primarily a set of techniques for satisfying needs, for problem solving, and for adjusting to the external environment" (Axelson, 1985, 4). These techniques are ways that the person in the culture has learned to meet the demands of the culture. Each person has a set of cultural techniques derived from the cultural group but screened through the individual's experience within that culture. These techniques may differ from person to person even in the family group. Kracke (1987, 49) reminds us that "Each person experiences similar situations quite differently. Certain situations call for identical responses from all cultural members, but feeling and personal ideas associated with the outward behaviors may differ from person to person, or people may integrate the patterns quite differently into their lives and overall persona." The responsibility of the social worker is to discover and learn from prospective clients their views on their cultural group and how they have responded to the cultural imperatives (Gray, Hartman & Saalberg, 1985).

To not consider the person's views on cultural materials is to not individualize the person. If the social worker has only an information bank of central tendency information, interpretations of interview content, behavior, and responses lead to a helping process based on the cultural imperatives of the social worker. This can result in misdiagnosis. It can also lead to judgments of the person's capacity to form a therapeutic relationship. The noted behaviors may be, and most often are, a manifestation of a cultural imperative on the part of the person. Content of an interview with a person of another ethnic cultural group can be misinterpreted as showing mental disturbance when in reality it is simply being expressed through culturally appropriate means. The content of the interview is best thought of as culturally meaningful expressions of problem-solving efforts.

Even though the extent of knowledge obtained by the social worker through formal educational paths is uneven across the entire educational system of social work, content is being offered to educate social workers regarding the history and impact of culture on growth and development of contrasting cultural groups being served by the social welfare system (Green, 1995; Slonim, 1991; Rothman, Gant, and Hnat, 1985; Whittaker and Tracy, 1989; Silva, 1983; Chestang, 1980). Such knowledge can be useful to assist the social worker in understanding the many cultural groups social workers serve and thus aid in the helping process. To avoid stereotyping the person through central tendency group information, the social worker is urged to consider the practice principle of "starting where the client is" by exploring the person's worldviews before making judgments based on group knowledge.

SELF-KNOWLEDGE

The importance of self-knowledge is not unknown. Knowing oneself has been a major theme of philosophy, poetry, psychology, psychiatry, the arts, and social work for many years.

In social work, self-knowledge and self-awareness issues surfaced as social work faced the issues involved in helping African Americans by considering the concept of race. In interracial helping situations, self-awareness was necessary because of the propensity of social workers to lose objectivity, accuracy, and sensitivity when working with African Americans. The social worker's countertransference was an important dynamic to manage (Lindsay, 1947; Brown, 1950).

Unconscious feelings and attitudes become activated in interracial situations and relationships. Because of these factors, social workers were more comfortable in discussing issues not related to race or minimized the racial issues in the interview content. The ability of social workers to openly acknowledge race as a factor in the helping process was questioned, and the highly charged issue of race could not be dealt with because of the countertransference of the social worker (Brown, 1950; Curry, 1964; Boyer, 1964; and Fibush, 1965). To manage racial issues adequately, social workers had to be aware of what race meant to them, the genesis of racial attitudes in society, how they managed cross-racial situations in the past, and the derivation of negative and positive racial inclinations from their own cultural and racial experiences toward specific racial groups and individuals.

Helpers not only bring academic knowledge and past helping experiences to bear on the problem solving efforts; they also bring themselves. How this self interacts with other selves becomes a major concern to all helping disciplines, including the profession of social work. Cecchin, Lane, and Ray (1994) urge helping professionals to become accountable by acknowledging the danger of their own preconceived notions and views. Social workers can inject self into a case situation as a result of their own family and cultural relationships and experiences. Before entering into the lives of ethnic minority persons, a social worker must understand his or her own drives and behavioral imperatives related to race and culture. Knowledge of self is essential for the conscious use of the relationship (Hamilton, 1967, 41). The use of self as the major instrument of helping the culturally contrasting person may be based on an awareness of how the self operates. Once the social worker has fine-tuned knowledge of self, acceptance and respect for others is possible.

When the person and the social worker meet in a professional encounter, neither has a clue to the outcome. The social worker wants to be successful, the person wants to be helped. But neither knows how they will relate and narrow the distance between them. The many variables such as culture, race, ethnicity, and gender may play a definitive part in whether the gap between the two can be bridged. In fact, the social worker's first task is to discover whether the contrasting variables can be bridged. If the social worker has no awareness of his or her reactions toward others, the distance between them will always be an issue (Young-Bruehl, 1996).

Each person in the helping encounter brings self in the present and self from the past. These present and past experiences must be understood by the social worker, as they can operate to either sabotage or aid the helping. Research studies focused on cross-cultural encounters reveal that most ethnic minority persons believe the major negative factor to be the insensitivity revealed in the behaviors and attitudes of the helper. This issue of relationship formation is highlighted when the helper and the person come from different cultural and racial backgrounds, as these factors may have a relationship to each other.

To be effective in cross-cultural practice, social workers must be (1) flexible in the use of self; (2) risk takers in the sense of being open to others even when they do not fully understand what they are being open to; and (3) empathic toward the minority position in society (Krajewski-Jaime et al., 1996). These traits are predicated on the ability of social workers to examine who they are, how they got that way, and how they think, act, and relate to others. Social workers must engage in activities that focus on the identification of their own "cultural trances." Allen-Agbro (1996) views cultural trances as inner forces that result from both individual and group cultural history and operate outside the person's conscious awareness. The social worker must break the cultural trance by "(1) identifying and exploring the deep culture that shapes behavior and worldviews, (2) learning interventions to transform one's relationship to culture, and (3) learning methods to transform one's relationship to the concept of culture" (Allen-Agbro, 1996). Through a process of examination, the social worker achieves a sense of self and can become more aware of self-attributes that may create barriers to effective relation formation and ongoing helping services.

Awareness of self on an honest level involving values, assumptions about people and life, and emotional reactions to problems and their presentation is necessary to free oneself to learn and use helping skills in the service of a person requesting help. Awareness of self as a cultural being is most important in cross-cultural work. What is the meaning of culture to individual social workers, and how has their culture made them the same in contrast to the ethnic minority persons whom they will serve professionally? It is vital to effective cross-cultural practice that this question be answered.

The achievement of self-awareness is an ongoing process, never finished. Avenues of approach to self-understanding and acceptance involve personal exploration of experiences to identify the attitudes, attributes, conceptions, and behaviors that derive from the social worker's place in society in formative years and in the present. The attainment of cultural competence can begin with the use of the exercises at the end of this chapter.

No helping person is immune to the imposition of personal worldviews on the helping process. "Know thyself" has been an axiom for centuries.

In cross-cultural practice, the social worker has to accept that any given culture is paramount to its possessor and alien to others. The ability to understand and work with others of a contrasting culture goes beyond mere civil behavior. Understanding is built on deep appreciation of the strength of culture in the lives of people. To overcome the tendency to look and act toward others on the basis of their own cultural framework and imperatives, social workers must understand themselves as cultural beings very much like the people they would help.

Self-awareness is a process both cognitive and emotional. The attainment of self-awareness is not easy but it is necessary. Social workers in direct practice with those of another culture need to have a firm grasp on self and an ability to look into self consistently. The process is important and adds to the knowledge base for effective cross-cultural practice.

EXERCISES

The following exercises will increase your understanding of the material presented in this chapter.

Exercise 1

1. Choose one ethnic minority group and develop a bibliography that could be useful in learning about the culture of the group. Explain why a particular reading would be helpful in developing understanding of and sensitivity to that group.
2. Select three areas of knowledge and relate them to African Americans, Asian Americans, Hispanics/Latinos, and Native Americans. For example, you might choose to explore cultural patterns of relating to outsiders or disciplining children.
3. Discuss your understanding of the central tendencies concept. What are the positives and negatives of this concept for cross-cultural practice?

Exercise 2   My Cultural Identity

Respond to items 1–5 with brief answers. Then discuss your answers with others in your small group.

1. Messages I got growing up from my mother about being a member of an ethnic group.
2. Messages I got from my father about being a member of an ethnic group.
3. Messages I got growing up from my extended family about socializing with or belonging to the dominant group or community.
4. Messages I got growing up from my extended family about marrying outside of my ethnic group.
5. Messages I got from my family about surviving in life as an ethnic person.

After sharing your answers, discuss the implications of your acculturation process for becoming an ethnically and culturally competent social worker.

Exercise 3   Problem Solving a Cold

As a child, each of us suffered from an occasional cold. Think back to your early years and the remedies your parents or parental figures used to combat colds.

1. Did the remedy cure your cold?
2. Have you used the same cold-solving remedies with children in your care?
3. Why or why not?

Consider the implications of this exercise in terms of how aspects of our cultures are passed from one generation to another.

Discuss this exercise as it relates to your thinking regarding culturally congruent treatment.

Exercise 4

On observation, some people of all races seem to have the ability to relate comfortably and effectively with others of a contrasting culture. Why is this so?

This brief exercise may assist you in assessing your own adaptive potential.

1. What is your race?
2. How do you think your race may effect your adaptive potential both positively and negatively (a) with members of another race and (b) with members of the same race?

Exercise 5   Racial Matters

The impact of the dominant culture and race on minority people of color must be considered a knowledge area for the culturally competent social worker. The attitudes and views about minority people of color are part of the dominant culture's thinking and impact the minority person of color's views of self and others. This exercise is presented to encourage your thinking and discussion of the elements of the dominant culture that have implication for your professional work.

1. It has been stated that the minority person of color must intersect with the dominant culture once the family is left.

   a. What are views of the dominant culture in regards to Native Americans? How are these views manifested?
   b. What are the views of the dominant culture in regards to African Americans? How are these views manifested?
   c. What are the views of the dominant culture in regards to Asian Americans? How are these views manifested?
   d. What are the views of the dominant culture in regards to Hispanic/Latino Americans? How are these views manifested?

2. Choose a major work of the dominant culture's literature in which a main character is a person of color and discuss the author's views of this person.
3. Consider the cultural area of music and explore how the contributions of minority persons of color have been accepted or rejected.
4. What are the dominant culture's views of minority women of color historically? Explore gender issues as related to minority women of color.
5. As a member of the dominant culture, consider how these views of minority people of color have impacted your views of people of color.
6. Discuss this statement with a small group of peers: *White people are shaped by their families, and minority people of color are shaped by encounters with the family and the surrounding environment.*

What are the implications of the discussion on the thrust toward equality in our society, on social policy, and on social services to minority populations of color?

REFERENCES

Allen-Agbro, Edree. (1996). Personal communication, May 14.
Axelson, John A. (1985). *Counseling and development in a multicultural society.* Monterey, CA: Brooks/Cole.

Boyer, Bryce. (1964). Psychoanalytic insights in working with ethnic minorities. *Social Casework, 45*(8), 519–526.

Breslin, Richard W., Cushner, Kenneth, Cherrie, Craig, & Young, Mahealani. (1986). *International interactions: A practical guide.* Beverly Hills, CA: Sage.

Brown, Luna. (1950). Race as a factor in establishing a casework relationship. *Journal of Social Casework, 32*(3), 91–97.

Cecchin, Gianfranco, Lane, Gerry, & Ray, Wendel A. (1994). *The cybernetics of prejudices in the practice of psychotherapy.* London: Karnac.

Chestang, Leon. (1980). Competencies and knowledge in clinical social work: A dual perspective. In Patricia Ewalt (Ed.), *Towards a definition of clinical social work* (pp. 1–22). Washington, DC: National Association of Social Work.

Cross, Terry, Barzron, Barbara J., Dennis, Karl W., & Isaacs, Mareasa R. (1989). *Towards a culturally competent system of care.* Washington, DC: Georgetown University Child Development Center.

Curry, Andrew. (1964). The Negro worker and the white client: A commentary on the treatment relationship. *Social Casework, 45*(3), 131–136.

English, Richard. (1984). *The challenge for mental health: Minorities and their world views.* Austin, TX: University of Texas Press.

Fibush, Esther. (1965). The white worker and the Negro client. *Social Casework, 46*(5), 271–277.

Fleming, Robert. (1996). *The wisdom of elders.* New York: Ballantine.

Gil, Rosa M. (1984, May 17). The ethnic patient: Implications for medical social work practice. In *Cross-cultural issues: Impact on social work practice in health care. Conference proceedings* (pp. 19–32). New York: Columbia University School of Social Work.

Gray, Sylvia Sims, Hartman, Ann, & Saalberg, Ellen S. (1985). *Empowering the black family.* Ann Arbor, MI: University of Michigan School of Social Work, National Child Welfare Training Center.

Green, James W. (1995). *Cultural awareness in the human services* (2nd ed.). Boston: Allyn & Bacon.

Hamilton, Gordon. (1967). *Theory and practice of social case work* (2nd ed.). New York: Columbia University Press.

Kleinman, Arthur. (1988). *Rethinking psychiatry: From cultural category to personal experience.* New York: The Free Press.

Kracke, Ward H. (1987). A psychoanalyst in the field: Erickson's contribution to anthropology. In Jerome Rabow, Gerald M. Platt, & Marion Goldman (Eds.), *Advances in psychoanalytic sociology.* Malabar, FL: Robert E. Krieger.

Krajewski-Jaime, Elvia R., Brown, Kaaren Strauch, Ziefert, Marjorie, & Kaufman, Elizabeth. (1996). Utilizing international clinical practice to build inter-cultural sensitivity in social work students. *Journal of Multicultural Social Work, 4*(2), 15–25.

Lewis, Harold. (1982). *The intellectual base for social work practice.* New York: The Haworth Press.

Lindsay, Isabel Burns. (1947). Race as a factor in the caseworker's role. *Journal of Social Casework, 28*(3), 101–107.

Rothman, Jack, Gant, Larry M., & Hnat, Stephen A. (1985, June). Mexican-American family culture. *Social Service Review, 59*(2), 197–215.

Silva, Juliette S. (1983). Cross-cultural and cross-ethnic assessment. In G. Gibson (Ed.), *Our kingdom stands on brittle glass* (pp. 59–66). Washington, DC: National Association of Social Workers.

Slonim, Maureen (1991). *Children, culture and ethnicity.* New York: Garland.

Talbert, Wynn, & Sullivan, Peggy. (1988). *Competency based child welfare practice: Research findings.* Fresno, CA: Child Welfare Training Project, CSU Fresno School of Health and Social Work.

Whittaker, James K., & Tracy, Elizabeth M. (1989). *Social treatment.* New York: Aldine DeGruyter.

Wilson, Linda. (1982). *The skills of ethnic competence.* Unpublished resource paper. Seattle: School of Social Work, University of Washington.

Young-Bruehl, Elisabeth. (1996). *The anatomy of prejudices.* Cambridge, MA: Harvard University Press.

5

THE HELPING RELATIONSHIP

Fixing pipes is complicated, fixing people is relatively simple provided the social worker can learn to take a helper's stance on the side of the experiential paradox.—ANDREW CURRY, 1973

For any helping encounter to be successful, a positive relationship has to be established between the social worker and the person. Rapport is having a close relationship characterized by harmony and agreement. A relationship must be developed that will "enable the interviewee to reveal essential facts of his situation and that will enable the interviewer to be most effective in helping" (Garrett, 1972, 6). Social workers strive to form the relationship that Perlman (1972) states is the heart of helping. Without a positive relationship, nothing constructive occurs. Forming the positive relationship is an act of faith, an element of hope, an unknown outcome of the helping encounter. It can be subject to time, opportunity, and chance. Therefore social workers need to be knowledgeable about the concepts of relationship and skillful in putting those concepts into practice.

The social worker needs to establish a relationship that will enable the person from a contrasting culture to experience acceptance and understanding as a necessary but not always sufficient condition of being helped. The person must perceive the social worker as well informed, capable, trustworthy, and credible—from the person's cultural viewpoint. The social worker needs to be highly accommodating to the other, but not to the extent that personal cultural integrity and identity are lost. The complexity of this dual identification causes most cross-cultural practice problems. Social workers can fear an identity and cultural loss by entering into a relationship in which they must be culturally accommodating.

In cross-cultural practice the formation of the relationship is probably the most troublesome worry. Referring to the perceptions of social workers and Chicano clients, Gomez and Becker (1985, 46) concluded that the major barrier in forming a relationship across cultures is a lack of cultural congruence that affects the communication process. The key to attaining cultural congruence is to "begin where the client is" rather than follow preset agency guidelines for interviewing. The social worker can find out where the client is culturally by using interviewing guidelines modeled on ethnographic procedures.

Many factors must be considered in cross-cultural practice. The knowledge, skills, and attitudes of the social worker are important elements in forming a helping relationship with a person of a contrasting culture. Social workers can learn about cultures, but knowledge must be translated into procedures that can be helpful in the interview. Conceptual knowledge by itself is not linked to particular procedures that result in effective helping because it is removed from the actual outcome of treatment (Sue & Zane, 1987). The social worker needs to focus on more immediate issues of relation formation and not rely on knowledge alone.

From a social science perspective, culture is brought to the encounter automatically by both parties. The person who needs help and the social worker are parts of "a number of subcultural reference groups and bring to the helping encounter perceptions and role expectations of the other that derive from their earlier memberships in a family that belonged to a certain subculture" (Kumabe, Nishida, & Hepworth, 1985, 31).

In traditional practice modalities, the person is expected to learn about the culture of helping in order to become a client. People are not clients but applicants for service until they have met the criteria for being clients. Alcabes and Jones (1985, 51) assert, "A significant portion of the initial interaction between a social worker and a new referral involves convincing the new referral, or applicant, that he or she needs the help the professional has to offer. Inherent in this process is teaching the applicant the norms appropriate to the status of client and gaining agreement that he or she will abide by these norms." The client is thus in the role of stranger to be acculturated into another culture.

In cross-cultural practice an opposite stance is argued. The social worker has a responsibility to learn about the other's culture first by crossing the cultural boundaries if an effective relationship is to be established. The social worker takes on the role of stranger, and the client becomes the cultural guide and teacher of his or her culture. Common ground must be established, and it is the social worker who must make the first effort to achieve the common ground.

In trying to establish a relationship, the social worker must keep in mind that cultural, racial, and ethnic contrasts will have a determining effect on the process. Launching into data gathering that is focused on the presenting problem may well be perceived as intrusive and disrespectful. Instead, the social worker in cross-cultural situations might display interest in family and friends, the achievement of family members, and discovering mutual friends and acquaintances. Time must be taken to develop the relationship or the relationship may never develop. In the ethnographic interviewing model, time is circular, not linear; it is wholly dependent on the process, not on the ends.

Language issues are involved in relationship formation. The social worker should not use technical jargon or terminology more appropriate to members of the professional culture than to the minority person of color. Language ought to be simple and follow the direction of the person as to pace and depth of communication. By a process congruent with the culture of the person, the social worker as stranger gets into the cultural flow easily. Saunders (1954, 8) states, "When persons of widely dissimilar or subcultural orientations are brought together in a therapeutic relationship, the probability of a mutually satisfactory outcome may be increased if those in the healing roles know something of their own culture and that of the patient and are aware of the extent to which behavior on both sides of the relationship is influenced by cultural factors." I would suggest that the social worker reconsider such guidelines in view of the social worker as stranger.

Ethnographic interviewing is presented as an avenue through which the social worker as stranger can be interested, sincere, and trustworthy by listening to the person's narrative as he or she becomes the social worker's cultural guide. The narrative can be instructive, as it is grounded in the culture of the client (Saaleby, 1994).

The roles of stranger and cultural guide become operationalized as the interview process steps are introduced. Knowledge of role transformation is important, but needed is a set of procedures that (1) allows for how individuals relate to others in ways culturally appropriate to themselves, and (2) recognizes that people can educate each other in a dialogue situation. The major process steps for interviews based on an ethnographic framework are as follows:

1. Formulating global questions
2. Asking global questions and listening for cover terms
3. Eliciting descriptors
4. Writing an ethnographic summary

When a translator is used, the process of interviewing a non-English-speaking person is identical to that of interviewing an English-speaking person.

With the parallel growth of minority populations of color and heightened awareness of multiculturalism and multilingualism in the United States, social services might expect to encounter many clients who do not speak or have proficiency in English. Being aware of this factor, the culturally competent social worker should be prepared to utilize the services of an interpreter for assistance in the interview process. *Merriam–Webster's Collegiate Dictionary* (10th ed., 1993) defines an interpreter as "one who translates orally for parties conversing in different languages." A good interpreter is proficient in both languages, is a skillful listener to words, and has the ability to translate not only those words but also their contextual meaning into the other language. The interpreter should understand both cultures in order to communicate the intent of the words spoken in the interview. One danger is that translators may give their own interpretation and wording to the words of another. In essence they are serving as a screen between cultures and have the potential to apply only their own meanings to the words spoken in either language.

Social work professionals must establish careful guidelines for the use of interpreters in delivering social services to non-English-speaking people. Freimanis (1994, 326) classifies interpreters into two major categories. The professional interpreter works mainly in the global arena for clients such as the United Nations or international corporations and may speak several languages. The community facilitator usually speaks only two languages, is often a volunteer, and rarely has received professional training as an interpreter. Social service agencies mainly use community facilitators from the minority group. Such persons, according to Freimanis (327), "cause problems not only because they lack skill but also because they may reflect the perceived social and educational level of the minority," which is viewed negatively by the social worker, the agency, and the society. Thus the community facilitator may have negative feelings about the social worker's culture and pass those feelings on to the minority person being interviewed or "make their cultural counterparts 'look better' in the eyes of the worker by altering or editing any questionable information given by the client" (328).

With the inclusion of a translator, the interview group becomes a triad in which a pairing may develop, leaving one person an outsider. Sharing the same language, the translator and the minority person may coalesce, and a trusting relationship between the minority person and the social worker becomes more difficult to develop. Therefore the translator must be viewed as a coequal in achieving the purposes of the interview. Prior to the interview, the interdependence of the social worker and the translator must be discussed and any possible barriers to the objectives of the interview acknowledged. The translator should be very familiar with the purposes and objectives of the interview and aware of the need for confidentiality and a nonjudgmental attitude regarding the information exchanged therein.

If a translator is to be used in an interview that follows ethnographic procedures, the translator should be trained in the purpose, process, and objectives of the model. The culturally competent social worker and the translator may rehearse the interview to learn the roles of each person. A rehearsal will provide the translator with experience in an interview where the purposes and objectives are different from other forms of interviewing. The rehearsal experience can elicit questions from the translator about the coming interview. The culturally competent social worker and the translator can enter into a dialogue that serves to establish a relationship between them. The translator accepts a role as an integral part of the interview, not just a conduit for transmitting information between the social worker and the client who speaks a language other than English. The translator becomes a cultural guide to both the social worker and the minority person in the process of the interview.

Ideally, the culturally competent social worker should be aware of issues involved when delivering social services to non-English-speaking culturally contrasting persons. In the education of social workers, practice courses with content related to contrasting cultural groups should introduce working with non-English-speaking persons. Practice role-playing would increase the student's learning, making social workers more aware of how to help those who do not speak English. How to work effectively with translators would be a useful part of social work education.

Linguistic differences will be encountered in social agencies of the future. Even after increasing the number of bilingual social workers, agencies will not have sufficient bilingual staff to meet this emerging need. The use of certified or professionally trained translators will be one option available to some agencies. Worth considering will be educational activities that attune the professionally trained translator to the mission, purpose, and practice of the social agency to minimize distortion of the information that will be screened through the translator.

THE PERSON AS A CULTURAL GUIDE

One of the most difficult tasks that people face in relating to those of another culture is developing a means of learning about one another. Reed (1988, 6) asserts that African American men view their lives as like being in a gym fighting impersonal opponents because they face hostility and rudeness of a society that fears and fascinates them. A social worker engaged in a helping process with African American men ought to know how they view themselves in a society, as this view may be very important to the problems they are seeking assistance to resolve. How can a social worker learn how people of contrasting cultures view their lives? Reed (6) is convinced that "it takes an extraordinary amount of effort to understand someone from a background different from your own, especially when your life really doesn't depend upon it." Dominant cultural groups need to understand that the lives of all people are mutually dependent and that the basis for this mutual dependency is understanding of the other.

Extraordinary effort by social workers entails self-disclosure through an admission that they know nothing (or know very little) about the lives of persons whose cultural, racial, and ethnic backgrounds are radically different from their own. For the social worker to admit ignorance of others' lives could be problematic because of the formal or informal education of social workers. Knowledge is taught about people by other professional people, not by the people themselves.

In working with Native Americans, for example, the social worker who is all-knowing will harm the relationship. Social workers who admit a lack of knowledge about Native Americans will be more respected than social workers who act as if they know (Lockart, 1981, 33).

The ethnographic interview process attempts to assist the social worker in rectifying this common teaching error by stating that a person is the expert on his or her life, and that if the social worker wishes to learn about that life, the person who experiences that life has to be the teacher.

The social worker initially self-discloses unfamiliarity with aspects of the person's cultural world. The social worker may also decide to self-disclose ignorance throughout the course of the interview, if such behavior will encourage the person to self-disclose by sharing information in that area.

Self-disclosure occurs when a person reveals something about self that is personal or would not be disclosed in random conversation (Dindia, 1995; Harvey, 1995; Hooks, 1994; and Ramsell & Ramsell, 1994). Self-disclosure appears more related to the situation itself than to any personality factors present in the person (Jourard & Jaffee, 1970, 253). Self-disclosure also occurs when the social worker admits a lack of knowledge or range of behaviors that prevent true culturally congruent responses or actions. Self-disclosure answers the person's question as to why the ethnographic interview process is going to followed in the interview.

Self-disclosure by the social worker demonstrates to the person a willingness to be open and to risk in the relationship. The social worker's self-disclosure will result in the self-disclosing behavior of the person. Jourard and Jaffee's (1970) study of the interview process indicates that if one wishes to invite disclosure from another, an effective means of doing so is to engage in the activity oneself. The social worker by self-disclosing models self-disclosure by setting an example of self-disclosing behavior.

The request for the person to become the cultural guide follows self-disclosure. When people begin to educate the social worker in aspects of their culture, they become the cultural guides or informants in ethnographic terminology. The social worker openly requests a person to assume this role at an appropriate time in the opening phase of the ethnographic interview and seeks open agreement to this suggestion. If the person refuses, the social worker will have to focus on discovering the basis for the refusal. The process of finding out from the person the initial barriers to communication may open the way for the person to enter into the beginning of a dialogue needed for effective helping. The following case example demonstrates this point.

SOCIAL WORKER: Hi, Anne. How are you today?

ANNE: Oh, pretty good.

SOCIAL WORKER: The principal told me you asked to speak with a social worker. He called me and then I sent you the note asking you to come in today. I see a lot of students here at the school, and I hope that I will able to help you out.

ANNE: I know. I heard a girl talk about coming to see the social worker. That is how I came to ask to talk with someone.

SOCIAL WORKER: What did you hear about us?

ANNE: Well, it was pretty good. I heard that she ate when she came in for her interviews and they talked about things that bothered her.

SOCIAL WORKER: How about a piece of this candy? (*Moves a dish filled with candy nearer to Anne*)

ANNE: (*Laughs*) She was right. (*Takes a piece of candy and looks around the office*) You have a nice place here. Are all the offices like this? Or did I draw a good hand?

SOCIAL WORKER: The offices are a little different from each other. I guess it depends on who is in them. If you would like, I can show you around.

ANNE: Maybe another time, but this office is okay.

SOCIAL WORKER: You know, Anne, you asked did you draw a good hand, and I was tempted to say "I think so." But then I thought I ought to find out what "a good hand" is all about. When people use words they have a reference to something in their world. For a person like me who does not know that world, it is important that I learn about that world. I have worked with some adult Native Americans but no teenagers. I am really a stranger to you. You can help me.

ANNE: I really have not heard about you, so I guess we are strangers.

SOCIAL WORKER: When two people are strangers they have to get to know each other and become one another's teacher. Would you be my teacher, like a guide into what your world is like?

ANNE: I don't know what to say, but I always wanted to teach. I can start now.

This social worker openly communicated that an exchange of knowledge was possible. Anne was an expert on her own life and the social worker was an expert on the professional experience. They could learn from each other. The person being helped becomes a cultural guide or informant, and the social worker becomes a learner.

A study of the history of cultural minority populations lends evidence to the willingness of minority persons to become cultural guides for cultural strangers. Through direct guidance to strangers or through oral or written narratives directed to dominant cultural populations, significant historical figures have accepted this role. They set an example for all those who wonder if minority cultural representatives are willing to take on the role of teacher.

A Native American woman named Sacagawea and an African American male, Frederick Douglass, are examples of minority persons who were cultural guides before the advent of anthropology and the concept of cultural guide. Sacagawea accompanied Meriwether Lewis and William Clark on their expedition to map the Northwest Territory granted to the United States in 1803 through the Louisiana Purchase. Sacagawea's knowledge of her culture, the land of her people, and adjacent Native American tribes proved invaluable to the expedition's eventual success (Sabin, 1917).

Taking on the role of cultural guide, Sacagawea instructed the strangers in aspects of Native American culture that enabled their survival in a hostile land where it was necessary to adapt to unfamiliar climate conditions, foods, language, and methods of relationship formation. She translated languages, taught them to use cultural symbols and meanings, and acted as a front person in initial contacts between the white expedition members and the various Native American tribes they encountered on the journey from the Midwest to the Pacific Ocean. Even more important, Sacagawea opened windows to the cultural world of the Native American tribes. Her presence as a cultural guide was her main role, undercutting the assumptions of the white expedition members that the territories held no civilized persons and that they were penetrating a foreign land two thousand miles in depth (Howard, 1971, 28). Such negative views of Native Americans and the land they occupied made situations ripe for disaster when the cultures met. Sacagawea's presence reassured the strangers that the cultural gaps would be bridged. She was more than a traveler looking for a home, and her role in U.S. westward development was more than that of an assistant (Howard, 1971, 149–151; Shoemaker, 1995, 11).

Frederick Douglass exemplifies the role of narrator as cultural guide. Endowed with extraordinary oratory gifts, a keen intelligence, and a capacity to be both of and outside the American culture of his time, Frederick Douglass became a cultural guide to the world of African Americans. His *Narrative of The Life of Frederick Douglass: An American Slave*, published in 1845, was praised as a self-revelation by a "man of noble proportions on which all Americans, white as well as black, might pattern themselves" (Andrews, 1996, 3). Frederick Douglass served as a cultural guide for the world into the life, the history, and the values of the nineteenth-century African American. He used his own story as a vehicle to educate strangers to the worldviews of his cultural and racial group. Particularly revealing was his account of the cruelty imposed on African American women and the impact of slavery on the physical and mental state of the African American family. Through the narrative form, Douglass fulfilled his "moral responsibility to report the ugliness imposed on African Americans by the ruling class" (Burke, 1996, 2). As a cultural guide, he dispelled the myths on which "tyrants have justified their tyranny by arguing the inferiority of their victims" (43).

Cultural guides serve as educators and informers by moving from the personal to the political realms of life in efforts to assist the stranger in listening to them and viewing the world through their eyes. Frederick Douglass's story exemplifies Fanon's observation (Young-Bruehl, 1996, 497):

> The basic experience of every Negro is to be caught between a Negro family and a white society, to be torn and traumatized by moving out of his family and into a scene where inevitably "a white man oppresses him with the whole weight of his blackness." The saving grace of this horror is that, for the Negro, the drama of race is never hidden and never repressed. The drama is there before his eyes, and conscious. The horror does not make him neurotic; even if it leaves him with a feeling of inferiority, that feeling is not unconscious. . . . The Negro can always tell—or sing, dance, or paint—his story.

From Douglass's day to this day, people of color continue to act as cultural guides through pride, through anger, through participation in a multicultural and multiracial country. A betrayal of the stories of cultural guides lies in taking the generosity of sharing and using it to further oppression and subjection. In cross-cultural encounters one teaches and one learns and both must listen.

The cultural guide or informant is a person who possesses special knowledge and is willing to share information of which the social worker is ignorant. The cultural guide "tells it as it is" from an insider's perspective and provides insights that the social worker does not have about cultural variables that impinge on the presenting problem. This is particularly apt in relation to values and value dilemmas in any cultural community. The social worker can gain a sensitivity to these value dilemmas through the teachings of the cultural guide or informant (Dean, Eichorn, & Dean, 1967).

The person in this phase of the ethnographic interview essentially agrees to become an informant. Because being an informant is a different role for many people, they may require time in the interview to consider whether they can or will perform it. "Informants are a source of information, literally they become teachers" (Spradley, 1979, 25). The informant is a person who is in the culture and is a teacher of the culture. The informant speaks the language of the culture and is subject to interrogation about the culture. The social worker reveals the aims of the questions, which are to learn about the other culture (Spradley, 1979).

For example, if a social worker is engaged with an African American who is a policeman and decides to use an ethnographic interview approach because little is known about the worldviews of African American policeman, the social worker might say, "I would like to learn about the life of an African American policeman. Your telling me about their experiences would be helpful to me in helping you and arriving at a successful conclusion to the problem you are having. I would be asking you some questions and writing down your answers." In this instance the social worker would be asking to learn about two cultural scenes: the life of an African American male and the life of an African American policeman.

The best informants are those who are acculturated in the sense that they know the culture well and have been a part of it for a lengthy period of time. Choosing as an informant a person who has just entered the cultural scene risks failure to learn intimate knowledge of the culture. The informant should also know that although the questioner is unknowing about the culture and cultural scenes, he or she will be learning through the information the informant offers. It is possible that those who think differently believe the social worker is dumb and only attempting to test them. The result may be a refusal to become a cultural guide.

Good informants use language to describe events and actions and offer analysis of events from an insider's point of view. For example, a student chose to learn about the culture of an agency. The informant agreed to be a teacher but could not talk the language of the agency. (The ability to translate one's culture into the culture of the other is not unusual for many ethnic minority persons who, for survival purposes, have learned to operate within the demands of the dominant culture.) Many persons seeking help attempt to explain themselves by relating to the culture of the helper rather than using their own cultural voice. This can create problems in the helping process. A good informant will describe the cultural scene in the language used in the culture, relating what the people did, how they did it, and how the people in the culture think about various matters (Spradley, 1979).

Once the social worker recognizes that the helping situation is characterized by the idea of cultural contrasts between the self and the other, the opportunity arises to make use of the cultural dimension. The social worker structures communication around ignorance of the other's culture and searches for communication procedures that will place him or her in a learning situation.

The ethnographic interviewing model is the appropriate interviewing model to achieve this objective. The social worker actively seeks a cultural guide in the person requesting help and, by using this person as an informant, attempts to discover ways of thinking about the culture as those elements of the culture relate to the presenting problem. Thus a tactical advantage develops out of the cultural dimension (Henson, 1983).

In working with an African American youth, one social worker explained to him that one purpose of the ethnographic interview was to obtain his point of view on problems African American youth had at the school. The social worker said, "I want to learn as much from you as I can about the boys and girls in this school and how they view the school and their place in it." This statement establishes specifically the kind of information wanted. It also asks the youth to be the social worker's cultural guide or teacher.

The cultural guide or informant concept can then be agreed on or not agreed on by the person. If it is agreed on, the social worker can return to statements during the course of the ethnographic interview that reinforce the cultural guide concept and the role of teacher, for example, "Would you repeat that? I want to be clear on what you are saying." Such statements said initially and interspersed throughout the interview, if necessary, reinforce the message and request. The social worker views the person as an expert with something to add to the cross-cultural encounter. The person is the cultural guide and, moreover, an expert on his or her life.

In actual practice there is no set formula for eliciting the cooperation of the person as cultural guide or informant, nor is there a definite time set to define a problem or focus the client in a certain direction (Thornton and Garrett, 1995, 69). Such decisions are left to the interviewer. How this occurs, and in what form, will depend on the personal style and comfort of the interviewer and may take a variety of forms. Consider the following.

1. In the initial interview with an Asian American adolescent, the social worker said, "You and I are beginning a journey together and for this journey I would like you to be my guide to the things boys like you do and think about. I will be asking you some questions that will help me learn, and you will respond as if I am the new boy on the block."

2. Another possible approach: "The interview we are going to have is to help me get a good understanding of the way your world works and how you view it from your perspective. That is really important as we begin to know each other. I need to get a big picture, and it's like you will draw the picture for me in words. Your words will teach me because I believe you are the expert on your world, not me. You know what it is like for you, and I am coming into that world fresh and I want to be sure that I can stand next to you and see things like you see them."

3. I told Mr. G. that I was interested in how his culture played a part in his life and wanted him to teach me about some aspects of family life on the reservation. Mr. G. said he was flattered that I was interested in Native Americans' views of the world and what they did on reservations. No one had ever asked him to explain his views, and he was quite willing to explain anything to me that I wanted to learn about.

4. In a second interview one social worker decided to change to an ethnographic interviewing mode and said to a Hispanic woman, "Today I want to do something different." When the Hispanic woman responded "Different?" the social worker said, "Yeah, like you being my teacher." The Hispanic woman pointed to herself and said, "Me, be a teacher?" The social worker said, "You know what your life is like for you and others like you better than anyone else. You can teach a lot about that life."

5. After an initial greeting one African American male said he was glad to be in the interview as he needed some help with the problems he had with his last girlfriend. He then went on to say that his friends were of no help and that he was a little nervous about being here as he did not know what to expect. The social worker stated that maybe both of them were nervous and did not know what to expect of each other. The social worker continued by suggesting that they begin with the African American male becoming his teacher to inform him how friends operate and what some of their thoughts might be about getting help. The social worker, without pause, continued by stating that he was asking the interviewee to tell his story as he saw it. The interviewee said that he was relieved, adding that his fear was that the social worker was going to tell him that his real problem was himself; but when he heard that the social worker wanted to hear about his life from his point of view that was great.

The following process also illustrates how to obtain a cultural guide for ethnographic purposes.

S.W.: Hi, Mr. Johnson. I'm glad to see you. Thank you for coming in today.

MR. J.: Well. I hope I can help you out. I just ate and I'm so shaky. I feel better when I eat. You know about that?

S.W.: I know when I am hungry how I feel. We may have the same reactions; we may not.

MR. J.: You may be right, something that fills me up can make someone else sick. Like I'm sleeping okay, better than a week ago. But the other guys here say they are sleeping worse. When I told them I was going to be your teacher about the guys here, they told me to be sure I told you about how they have to learn to sleep with noise.

S.W.: How many guys do you talk to in one day?

MR. J.: In one day? About fifteen to twenty. I bet you talk to a lot more every day.

S.W.: Depends on the day, but between us we see a lot of people with no place to live.

MR. J.: Yeah. I bet this office has seen a lot of things.

S.W.: Yeah. I don't know much, though, about the guys' lives every day, and it would help them if I could learn what a day in their life may be like. I'd like you, if you are willing, to tell me about how the life of your friends goes on. That means you will be a teacher.

MR. J.: (*Interrupting*) I don't know I know anything to teach, you know.

S.W.: Let's see. How long have you been traveling around the country living like you do?

MR. J.: Off and on for forty years.

S.W.: Would you say that you have met a lot of people living like you do?

MR. J.: Hundreds, all over the country.

S.W.: Those hundreds hold ideas and develop ways of doing things and seeing things unique to themselves. Those experiences are different from other people's. How much experience do you think I might have living the lifestyle that you have lived these forty years?

MR. J.: Almost none. (*Laughs*)

S.W.: Like I say, of the two of us, you are the expert in an area of life I know nothing about.

MR. J.: Well, putting it that way, you are right. I can teach you. (*Laughs*) Now what do you need to learn? (*Sits up straight; picks up a pencil*)

S.W.: How to make a shelter if two people need to stay outside at night.

MR. J.: The guys use anything handy . . .

THE SOCIAL WORKER AS STRANGER

The major role of the social worker in the ethnographic interview is that of stranger. If one considers that the social worker comes to the interview to discover the cultural imperatives of the culturally contrasting person, then in actuality the social worker comes to the encounter as a stranger. The social worker is very much like a person in the balcony watching others enact a play. To be helpful, the social worker must find a way to enter into the actors' social scenes. However, his or her thinking as usual will not stand the test of the play that must be joined. The social worker does not know the plot, the language, or the actors well enough to become an equal player.

Social workers have been asked to assume many roles in the course of a helping process: counselor, advocate, friend, therapist, resource finder, teacher, consultant. While these roles are important to helping procedures, in the ethnographic model they are appropriate only after the social worker truly understands the worldviews and cultural imperatives of the person to be helped. It is by these rules that the action is governed.

In the beginning of a helping contact, one does not understand the cultural imperatives from the individual's perspective and therefore is a stranger to the culture. The stranger role must be accepted and conceptually understood by the social worker as a central role in the ethnographic interview model. This role has not been discussed in the social work literature, but its dynamics can be understood by considering the work of George Simmel (1980). An early sociologist, Simmel studied the dynamics of encounters between two individuals who do not know each other. When two persons first come together they are strangers, and neither is a part of the other's culture.

In the process they begin to share information—sometimes of a very confidential nature—that they might not share with another person in their culture. They confess to each other in the process of getting to know each other. They take risks with information giving. Since either person has the power to veto the other or withdraw from the relationship, both are under pressure to behave in such a manner that the other will not withdraw and will continue to cooperate even if it means a point has to be conceded at any time.

In a dyad one person will gravitate more toward giving information, while the other will be passive and agree more. These roles can shift depending on the dynamics of the encounter. At other times being a stranger can be inhibiting to both persons. When a stranger is confronted with something new, a defensive posture can ensue. There seems to be a threat, perhaps coming from the idea of a new association, new ideas, or new views on aspects of the world. Perhaps the most telling dynamic of the defensive posture is that there is uncertainty in the role needed to engage in relationship formation.

The stranger is a person who attempts to become accepted by a group that has adopted a scheme of cultural patterns handed down over generations and unquestioned for all situations that can occur in its social world. The stranger does not have knowledge of this scheme of cultural patterns. According to Schuetz (1960, 103), the stranger has to question and be informed about nearly everything related to the other's culture. Being a newcomer to the culture, the stranger is a person without a history in that world. The social worker is much like a person marrying into another family or a sojourner in another country.

Schuetz (1960, 105) refers to the stranger having as a first task the collecting of information before being able to think or act congruently with the unknown culture. Language is the medium through which the information is obtained. Language is more than just dictionary definitions or rules of grammar; it has meaning derived from the social environment within which it is used. Language includes technical terms, jargon, and dialects, the use of which is restricted to the inner group. Language has its own private code understandable to those who have participated in common past experiences. Language mirrors the history of the group and is manifest in its literature either oral or written. Prior to engagement with the people of another culture, the stranger might become familiar with its written literature, thereby gaining some knowledge of the group's language and worldviews.

Members of the cultural group neither question nor test the language scheme, usage, or meanings. It is their recipe for living but a mystery for the stranger. The stranger must first define the situation, however loosely, before asking questions or clarifying statements to discover the what and the why.

Being the stranger means being involved in a discovery process occurring in a field of adventure. Thinking as usual must be suspended. The journey into the cultural world of another, if successful, will result in the adoption of and adaptation to a view of the world no longer questionable; the patterns will become a matter of course no longer alien, strange, and foreign. The stranger becomes a part of the culture and is no longer a stranger.

In the ethnographic model of interviewing, the beginning role, taken with full awareness of the social worker, is that of stranger. The social worker as outsider rather than insider is a necessary alteration and difficult for most social workers to assume, as they have not been educated to techniques that place the person in the stranger role. Social workers are educated for the role of cultural gatekeeper and socialization conduit into the culture of helping. In the role of stranger, social workers do not know what they do not know. They find out what they do not know in the process of helping.

In general, social workers working cross-culturally are strangers to the culture of the other and may develop defensive postures that result in negative evaluations of the person. This may be particularly true when racial contrasts are also present. Assuming the role of stranger will work against negative evaluations. To achieve the central objective of learning and relationship formation, the social worker must assume the role of stranger in the cross cultural encounter. Through the development of ethnographic interviewing concepts and procedures, the social worker will have a framework for demonstrating the role of learner. Then one can learn what needs to be done and planned for based on what ethnic minority persons do in everyday life and think about why it is done to solve problems from the perspective of their own culture (Mitchell, 1982, 42).

EXERCISES

The following exercises will enhance your understanding of the material in this chapter.

Exercise 1

This assignment is designed to assist you in recognizing your process in securing a cultural guide or informant.

1. Locate one person from each of the following categories: a child between the ages of 7 and 11; an adolescent; an adult; an elderly person.
2. With each person engage in a conversation designed to enlist their cooperation as your cultural guide or informant.
3. Write a process recording of your conversation with each person.
4. Critique your communication regarding words used, your comfort level, and the response of the person.

Exercise 2

1. Expressing ignorance. Consider your family background, your culture, your life experiences, your inclinations and your values in relation to the word "ignorance." Write your thoughts down and consider how they affect your being able to express ignorance to a person in a professional encounter.
2. Discuss the adage "Ignorance is bliss." Is it or is it not?

Exercise 3   Evaluating Myself as a Cultural Guide

Everyone has been a cultural guide to someone else. This exercise is to assist you in deciding on the cultural areas of your life that you would be willing to teach to someone outside your cultural group. As one teaches, one self-discloses to others.

Please check your willingness or unwillingness to self-disclose in the following areas.

		Willing	*Unwilling*
1.	The thinking of my cultural group regarding outsiders	_____	_____
2.	The sexual values of my cultural group	_____	_____
3.	The role of females in my group	_____	_____
4.	Child-rearing patterns in my group	_____	_____
5.	How to dress in my cultural group	_____	_____
6.	The way my group dances	_____	_____
7.	The political preferences of my group	_____	_____
8.	My group's thinking about race	_____	_____
9.	How my group engages in racist practices	_____	_____
10.	My group's opinion about homosexuals	_____	_____
11.	My group's feelings about its place in society	_____	_____
12.	The roles of men in my group	_____	_____
13.	Things my group considers as group secrets	_____	_____
14.	My group's favorite music	_____	_____
15.	My group's thinking about sexual adequacies	_____	_____
16.	My disappointments with the opposite sex	_____	_____
17.	My opinion on marrying for money	_____	_____
18.	How often I have sexual experiences	_____	_____
19.	Radio and TV shows I watch	_____	_____
20.	Characteristics of my parents I dislike	_____	_____
21.	The foods my group eats	_____	_____
22.	Places where I work and live	_____	_____
23.	Aspects of my personality that I dislike	_____	_____
24.	How I feel about older persons	_____	_____
25.	My group's feelings about older persons	_____	_____
	Total number of willing areas	_____	_____
	Total number of unwilling areas	_____	_____

Examine your areas of willingness and unwillingness.

The areas can be grouped into two major themes: those that concern your cultural group and those that concern yourself.

In which theme area are you more willing to self-disclose?

In which theme area are you less willing to self-disclose?

From your findings in this exercise, what are the implications for your being open with outsiders?

Under what conditions may you self-disclose even when you think you are unwilling to self-disclose?

Exercise 4 Evaluating Myself as an Informant

An informant is a person who can speak in the language of his or her cultural group. The informant becomes a model for the stranger to emulate as the stranger moves into the culture of the informant. Informants are ordinary people doing ordinary things that people do every day.

An informant is a person who has been acculturated into a specific cultural group. Acculturation is the process of being conditioned to the patterns and customs of a culture. Every person in American society has been subject to acculturation into some cultural group. This brief exercise will help you think of yourself as an informant for a stranger to your cultural group.

Answer the following:

1. The cultural group to which I belong and would be willing to educate a stranger about is:

2. The length of time I have been in my cultural group is:

   Less than one year _____   More than one year _____

3. My ability to speak the language of my cultural group is:

   Good _____   Not so good _____

4. I am currently involved in the cultural group identified in question 1.

   Yes _____   No _____

5. I would be willing to be interviewed as an informant on my cultural group.

   Yes _____   No _____

6. I would be a good informant because:

7. Other cultural groups or scenes on which I am willing to be an informant are:

Exercise 5 Entering a New Culture

You have just received a one-year assignment to work for your child welfare agency in Haiti. You will work in the area of foster care and adoptions in the countryside surrounding Port-au-Prince. You have not been to Haiti before and know nothing about the country or its people.

1. What are some of the areas you might want to become knowledgeable about in the six weeks prior to leaving the United States?
2. What activities might you want to engage in prior to leaving the United States?
3. Once you arrive in Haiti, what will you do?
4. If you do prepare yourself for entry into the Haitian culture, what can you guess will happen?

Exercise 6   *Choosing a Community Interpreter*

The following statements refer to the skills and abilities of interpreters who serve non-English-speaking clients in settings such as social agencies, hospitals and mental health facilities. Assume you are selecting and/or training individuals who speak two or more languages, and who are not professional interpreters, to assume that role and act as communication facilitators. Please circle the option that best represents your opinion.

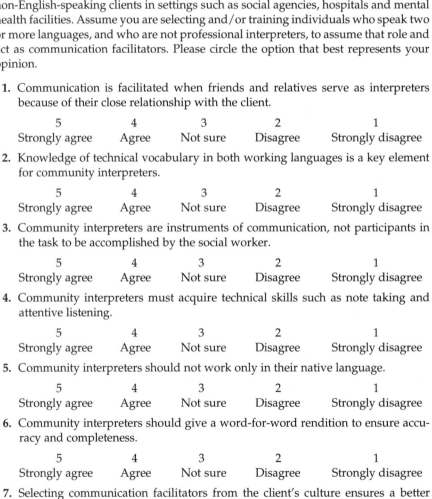

1. Communication is facilitated when friends and relatives serve as interpreters because of their close relationship with the client.

5	4	3	2	1
Strongly agree	Agree	Not sure	Disagree	Strongly disagree

2. Knowledge of technical vocabulary in both working languages is a key element for community interpreters.

5	4	3	2	1
Strongly agree	Agree	Not sure	Disagree	Strongly disagree

3. Community interpreters are instruments of communication, not participants in the task to be accomplished by the social worker.

5	4	3	2	1
Strongly agree	Agree	Not sure	Disagree	Strongly disagree

4. Community interpreters must acquire technical skills such as note taking and attentive listening.

5	4	3	2	1
Strongly agree	Agree	Not sure	Disagree	Strongly disagree

5. Community interpreters should not work only in their native language.

5	4	3	2	1
Strongly agree	Agree	Not sure	Disagree	Strongly disagree

6. Community interpreters should give a word-for-word rendition to ensure accuracy and completeness.

5	4	3	2	1
Strongly agree	Agree	Not sure	Disagree	Strongly disagree

7. Selecting communication facilitators from the client's culture ensures a better communication.

5	4	3	2	1
Strongly agree	Agree	Not sure	Disagree	Strongly disagree

8. Community interpreters should not intervene in the exchange between the social worker and the client.

5	4	3	2	1
Strongly agree	Agree	Not sure	Disagree	Strongly disagree

9. Community interpreters are usually volunteers.

5	4	3	2	1
Strongly agree	Agree	Not sure	Disagree	Strongly disagree

10. Most individuals who speak two languages have the skills to become good community interpreters.

5	4	3	2	1
Strongly agree	Agree	Not sure	Disagree	Strongly disagree

11. Community interpreters may benefit greatly by participating in rehearsal interview sessions.

5	4	3	2	1
Strongly agree	Agree	Not sure	Disagree	Strongly disagree

12. It is unrealistic to expect a good interpretation between languages with different grammatical structures.

5	4	3	2	1
Strongly agree	Agree	Not sure	Disagree	Strongly disagree

13. The community interpreter must become part of the treatment team.

5	4	3	2	1
Strongly agree	Agree	Not sure	Disagree	Strongly disagree

14. The community interpreter should be involved in all aspects of the helping process.

5	4	3	2	1
Strongly agree	Agree	Not sure	Disagree	Strongly disagree

Compare the chosen options with others in a small group and discuss the variables in utilizing and/or training of community interpreters (Freimanis, 1994).

REFERENCES

Alcabes, Abraham & Jones, James A. (1985). Structural determinants of "clienthood." *Social Work, 30*(1), 49–53.

Andrews, William L. (Ed.). (1996). *The Oxford Frederick Douglass reader.* New York: Oxford University Press.

Burke, Ronald K. (1996). *Frederick Douglass: Crusading orator for human rights.* New York: Garland.

Curry, Andrew. (1973). *Bringing forth forms.* Paradise, CA: Dustbooks.

Dean, John P., Eichorn, Robert L., & Dean, Lois R. (1967). Observation and interviewing. In T. Doby (Ed.), *An introduction to social research* (pp. 274–304). New York: Meredith.

Dindia, Kathryn. (1995). Self-disclosure: A sense of balance. *Contemporary Psychology,* *40*(1), 17–18.

Freimanis, Carolina. (1994). Training bilinguals to interpret in the community. In Richard W. Breslin & Tomoko Yoshida (Eds.), *Improving intercultural interactions: Modules for cross-cultural training programs.* Thousand Oaks, CA: Sage.

Garrett, Annette Marie. (1972). *Interviewing: Its principles and methods* (rev. 2nd edition by Elinor P. Zaki & Margaret M. Mangold). New York: Family Association of America.

Gomez, Ernesto, & Becker, Roy E. (1985). Comparisons between the perceptions of human service workers and Chicano clients. *Social Thought, 11*(3), 40–48.

Harvey, Aminifu. (1995). The issue of skin color in psychotherapy with African Americans. *Families in Society, 76*(1), 3–10.

Henson, James. (1983). *Cultural perspectives in family therapy.* Rockville, MD: Aspen Systems Corp.

Hooks, Bell. (1994). *Teaching to transgress.* New York: Routledge.

Howard, Harold P. (1971). *Sacagawea.* Norman, OK: University of Oklahoma Press.

Jourard, Sidney M., & Jaffee, Peggy E. (1970). Influence of an interviewer's self-disclosure on the self-disclosing behavior of interviewees. *Journal of Consulting Psychology, 17*(3), 252–257.

Kumabe, Kazuye T., Nishida, Chikae, & Hepworth, Dean H. (1985). *Bridging ethnocultural diversity in social work and health.* Honolulu, HI: University of Hawaii School of Social Work.

Lockart, Barbetta. (1981). Historic distrust and the counseling of American Indians and Alaska natives. *White Cloud Journal, 2*(3), 31–34.

Mitchell, Jacqueline. (1982). Reflections of a black social scientist: Some struggles, some hopes. *Harvard Educational Review, 52*(1), 27–44.

Perlman, Helen Harris. (1972). *Relationship: The heart of helping.* Chicago: University of Chicago Press.

Ramsell, Penny Smith, & Ramsell, Earle R. (1994). Counselor and client perceptions of the effect of social and physical contact on the therapeutic process. *Clinical Social Work Journal, 22*(1), 91–104.

Reed, Ishmeal. (1988). *Writin' is fightin'.* New York: Athenaeum.

Saaleby, Dennis. (1994). Culture, theory and narrative: The intersection of meaning in social work. *Social Work, 39*(4), 351–359.

Sabin, Edwin. (1917). *Opening the west with Lewis and Clark.* Philadelphia: Lippincott.

Saunders, Lyle. (1954). *Cultural differences and medical care.* New York: Russell Sage Foundation.

Schuetz, Alfred. (1960). The stranger: An essay in social psychology. In Maurice R. Stein, Arthur J. Vidich, & David Manning White (Eds.), *Identity and anxiety* (pp. 98–109). Glencoe, IL: The Free Press.

Shoemaker, Nancy. (1995, Summer). Native American women in history. *OAH Magazine of History,* pp. 10–14.

Simmel, George. (1980). The stranger. In Kurt Wolfe (Ed.), *The sociology of George Simmel* (pp. 402–409). Glencoe, IL: The Free Press.

Spradley, James. (1979). *The ethnographic interview.* New York: Rinehart and Winston.

Sue, Stanley, & Zane, Nolan. (1987). The role of culture and cultural techniques in psychotherapy: A critique and reformulation. *American Psychologist, 42*(1), 37–45.

Thornton, Serene, & Garrett, Kendra J. (1995). Ethnography as a bridge to multi-cultural practice. *Journal of Social Work Education, 31*(6), 67–74.

Young-Bruehl, Elisabeth. (1996). *The anatomy of prejudices.* Cambridge, MA: Harvard University Press.

6

FRIENDLY CONVERSATION

*You spend all this time with what sounds
like chit-chat, but it is not chit-chat.
It is really establishing who you are,
and I think that is very important.*
—*BARBARA SOLOMON, 1985*

A social worker must keep in mind that whether a person first comes to the interview situation voluntarily or involuntarily, the initial contact may begin with overt indicators of anxiety about what is going to happen and questions about the process to be followed. The initial focus of attention should be characterized by honest explanations and reassurance that such concerns and questions are entirely normal.

It is a rare interview that begins without an exchange of introductory remarks between the parties, yet little attention is given to a discussion of these remarks (Brammer, 1973, 58). The ethnographic interview process enables the person being interviewed to begin to know the social worker through friendly conversation.

No matter what the interview is to focus on, the initial communication should demonstrate that the interview situation will be one in which the person to be helped is welcome and respected. In most situations the natural conversation openers are regarded by social workers as preliminaries that ought to be focused quickly on the reasons why the person is at the interview. Prolonged conversation is viewed as the behavior of a person who is attempting either to avoid the problem or to deal with anxiety.

In the ethnographic interview the natural opening conversation is taken seriously. The purpose of friendly conversation is to begin the relationship not as a client or as a social worker but essentially as two people coming together to get to know each other. The social worker ought to consider the value of friendly conversation as a way to create a climate of acceptance and to give the client an opportunity to hear the social worker's voice as well as to experience the social worker as a human being.

Friendly conversation can be viewed as small talk. Benjamin (1974, 13) states that "sometimes there is room for small talk on the interviewer's part, something to help the interviewer get started."

Brief statements may break the ice: "With the traffic as it is around here, you must have found it hard to get a parking space!" or "It's nice to have a sunny day after all that rain, isn't it?" The suggestion is that the interviewer take the lead in the small talk, but on some occasions the person might introduce small talk, and the interviewer ought to respond.

As expansion on the idea of small talk, the initial conversation can be viewed as general conversation. Kadushin (1972) views preliminary conversation as chit-chat about any topic such as the weather, sports, or the current social event in the community. General conversation serves the purpose of easing the client into a new and unfamiliar mode of conversational interaction with which he or she may not be familiar, and it has the advantage of helping the person experience the humanness of the social worker.

From a cross-cultural perspective, the social worker needs to understand that the interview has a cultural base in the professional education of the social worker. The person interviewed is entering into that culture with its specific language, norms of behavior, and ethical stances. In an effort to assist the person interviewed in making that necessary cultural transition, the social worker can become skillful at the art of friendly conversation. The use of friendly conversation can help potential clients understand how the agency will approach them. It can also help them evaluate the social worker as the formation of the professional relationship begins.

In cross-cultural situations, the culturally relevant ways in which relationships are formed may do much to inform the social worker about acceptable areas of conversation and culturally appropriate topics in the early stages of relationship formation. Friendly conversation can be an entry point into this cultural knowledge.

Social workers should spend considerable time enhancing relationship skills, as relationships are the heart of helping (Perlman, 1972). Because of this, it is suggested that friendly conversation be considered crucial in cross-cultural interview situations.

In working with African Americans, the issue of establishing relationships early in the helping process is advanced. Solomon (1976, 320) speaks to the idea of authenticity as a necessary factor that occurs when the social worker is able to get inside the texture of African American life. Once social workers view life from the insider's perspective, then they can be authentic. The issue is achieving the point in the process at which the social worker can view the life of the African American from the perspective of the African American. Ethnographic interviewing is suggested as a skill that, if mastered, holds promise for the achievement of this goal.

Gibbs (1985, 184–195) addresses the issue of relationship building with African Americans through an analysis of her work as a consultant with African Americans. Gibbs outlines five steps of relationship building: (1) appraisal, (2) investigation, (3) involvement, (4) commitment, and (5) engagement. The art of friendly conversation is important to the first stage.

In the appraisal stage, the African American sits back and sizes up the social worker. This person may not be committed to the encounter, and behaviors of aloofness, reservation, and superficial pleasantry may be in evidence. Beneath this demeanor may be feelings of anxiety, distrust, suspicion, or hostility toward the social worker. The African American is evaluating the social worker's ability to be genuine and approachable. If the social worker does not impress the African American as a person with these traits, then the helping will have considerable obstacles in the path of problem resolution.

Friendly conversation may be an effective avenue to initially demonstrate to the person the social worker's interest in him or her and the social worker's humanness. Gibbs suggests that the social worker take on the orientation of interpersonal relationships prior to any work on the problem or task that is the focus of the encounter. People from minority cultures may personalize relationships that are considered impersonal to members of the dominant culture. This may be necessary with other culturally contrasting groups. Abad, Ramos, & Boyce (1974, 584–595) describe the concept of *personalismo* as the inclination of Latin people, in general, to relate to and trust persons rather than institutions. The professional relationship is viewed by most professional social workers as an impersonal one in which friendliness and mutuality play a minor part.

Friendly conversation is not considered an essential part of the ethnographic interviewing process, as it is not focused on obtaining culturally relevant information from the cultural guide. In fact, the person has not assumed the role of cultural guide during the stage of friendly conversation. But friendly conversation can set the stage for the person's willingness to become the social worker's cultural guide.

Spradley delineates elements of the friendly conversation:

1. *Greeting.* A verbal marker starts the friendly conversation such as hi, hello or a physical contact such as a handshake or hug. Whatever the form of greeting, it has a cultural base. The social worker needs to be aware of the cultural forms of greeting and respond appropriately. A non-verbal greeting indicates a closeness in the

relationship and may be used only after a relationship has been established.

2. *Lack of explicit purpose.* In friendly conversation no agendas are present. Either person can bring up a subject they want; either person can change the subject and either person can end the conversation.

3. *Avoiding repetition.* One important rule of friendly conversation is to avoid repetition. Checking to see if you have told the other about an event or thought is often done, for example, by saying "Did I tell you about my trip?" This gives the other person an opportunity to save the speaker from being embarrassed. In addition one person does not ask for detailed clarification of the other's statements.

4. *Asking questions.* In friendly conversation one can ask questions of the other person which allow personal matters to be talked about if the other person wishes to disclose material of a personal nature. The other person also has a reciprocal freedom to ask questions of a personal nature.

5. *Expressing interest.* Questions themselves indicate interest in the other person. Non-verbal interest is frequently shown by smiling and various body postures which say to the person that the other finds what they are saying interesting. These non-verbal expressions have a cultural base and the social worker would have to be certain that the non-verbal behaviors are viewed as culturally acceptable to the other person.

6. *Expressing ignorance.* To maintain the friendly conversation, expressions of ignorance are necessary. One can express ignorance either by language or body posture that encourages the other person to go on talking. For example, language expressions of ignorance would be, "I have never been to a soul food dinner" or "How do you prepare beans and rice?"

7. *Taking turns.* A cultural rule for friendly conversation is to take turns talking. Both persons must contribute something to the ongoing conversation. If not, a feeling of uneasiness or boredom may set in and this can lead to a cessation of conversation.

8. *Abbreviating.* Friendly conversations are filled with references that hint at other things or only give partial information. An economy of words is the rule. One lets the other fill in the gaps. This abbreviated conversation makes it extremely difficult for someone outside the conversation to know what is going on or what information is being transmitted.

9. *Pausing.* Brief periods of silence can occur when either person feels like not talking. Pauses can mean many things to the person in a conversation with another. It may mean the participants are gathering thoughts. It may mean the conversation is nearing an end. It may mean the topic is about to be changed. Either person can break a pause.

10. *Leave taking.* Friendly conversations stop with some ritualistic behavior. The participants must account for what they are about to do—stop talking. One does not say: "I do not want to talk to you anymore." One must give a socially acceptable way of ending. These endings vary by cultures. In some cultural groups phrases are used like "See you later," "Let's do lunch" or "Call me sometime." (1979, 56–58)

The following speech event, according to Spradley, is indicative of friendly conversation:

BOB: Hi, Fred! How are you? (*Bob extends his hand while Fred hurriedly shifts a package to his left hand so he can respond.*)

FRED: Fine. It's good to see you. (*A firm handshake is now underway, one that goes on for several seconds as they continue to talk.*)

BOB: How's the family? I haven't seen you since March. Did you have a good summer?

FRED: They're all doing fine. Jean left for college a few weeks ago.

BOB: That's right! How does it feel to have your oldest gone? Hardly seems possible. Billy's talking about the University of North Carolina for next year.

FRED: Did you have a good summer?

BOB: Well things were pretty hectic at the office. We did get away for a couple weeks to the Smokies. Then Barbara and I had a long weekend up in D.C.

FRED: The Smokies? That sounds great. We've never been to that part of the country.

BOB: It was beautiful. But hot in August. We camped out for part of the time. If we go again I think we'd try to make it in September, maybe even after the leaves have started to turn. How about you? Did you get away?

FRED: Yes, we spent three weeks in July up in Wisconsin.

BOB: Really! Where did you stay?

FRED: Rented a cabin up in the northwest corner of the state. Did a lot of fishing. Best time was canoeing on the Brule River—nice rapids, but not too much for the kids. Had to rent two canoes, but we spent several days doing that river.

BOB: What kind of fish did you get?

FRED: Bass, mostly, and panfish. John caught a musky and I think I had a northern pike on my line but he got away.

BOB: Say, how are things at the company?

FRED: In May Al was transferred to Fort Lauderdale and that took a lot of pressure off. And since then sales have been up, too. Had a really productive week in early June—all the field men came in and I think that helped. How about you, still thinking of a transfer?

BOB: Well, they keep talking about it. I've told them I'd rather wait till Danny finishes high school, but I don't think I could turn down a regional if it came along.

FRED: Look, I've got to meet Joan up the street in a few minutes; I'd better be off. It was really good to see you.

BOB: Yeah, let's get together sometime. I know Barbara would love to see Joan.

FRED: O.K. Sounds good. Take it easy now.

BOB: You too. Have a good day. (1979, 55–56)

It is not difficult to recognize this exchange as a friendly conversation. In evidence is the greeting, the casual nature of the speech, the speech acts used, and the cultural rules followed.

An interview is a particular kind of speech event. In our society many social occasions are identified by the kind of talking that takes place. We all recognize a sales pitch, a job interview, a friendly interaction or a monologue by the manner in which the talking occurs.

In social work practice a particular kind of talking occurs, but in many instances friendly conversation begins, ends, and is interspersed throughout the interview. In fact the social work interview can be conceptualized as a process beginning with friendly conversation and progressing to a form of talking that characterizes the helping interview.

Friendly conversation becomes a skill in establishing a positive relationship with a person of another culture. The length of time for friendly conversation depends on the interviewer assessing the level of comfort and ease of the other person in the encounter.

The value of friendly conversation is not to be underestimated in settling into an interview, in creating a working alliance, or in establishing trust. The content of the friendly conversation stage of the interview would depend on the circumstances present. The social worker and the client may share food as they talk. When the interview occurs in the home, opportunity may be present to talk about a TV show, an arrangement on the wall, or the furniture. The social worker may take the lead or the person may take the lead. The objective of friendly conversation is to set a tone of acceptance, interest, and respect for the person. If the social worker stays too long on friendly conversation, the person can become anxious. The ability to sense when the interview should move ahead can be learned through consideration of friendly conversation as a definitive part of the interview.

The first interview is to provide essential information for the helping process. But the process cannot begin until the social worker and the person have entered into a discourse through which the person begins to experience the social worker as someone who is genuinely interested in him or her as a person with a problem. Friendly conversation begins the formation of the working alliance. If the first interview is managed appropriately and sensitively, the social worker will have begun the process of bridging the existing cultural gap.

Topics of friendly conversation, especially in initial encounters where little relationship history exists, appear banal and innocuous. Examples are how one feels, the weather, and sports events. Friendly conversations at the beginning of the professional interview serve to get the session started.

Social workers who regularly interview persons of another culture ought to familiarize themselves with the other's manner of opening conversations. Clients may offer culturally appropriate ways of beginning relationships, enabling social workers to begin the learning process and enter into their clients' culture immediately. Experimenting with culturally specific conversational openers before learning what the conversational and relationship norms are should be done cautiously. Expressing ignorance about them and what they mean might be one way of building conversational currency.

Friendly conversation provides an avenue for social workers to begin to develop rapport with persons of a contrasting culture. Vontress (1971, 7) defines rapport as "comfortable and unrestrained relationship of mutual trust and confidence between two or more individuals" and "the existence of mutual responsiveness which encourages each member to react immediately, spontaneously, and sympathetically to the other." Familiarity with the cultural patterns of a person's life can be demonstrated during the phase of friendly conversation and may be very important in establishing rapport.

For example, if a social worker who belongs to the majority population is beginning to relate to an African American, he or she can learn about the African American's interests through friendly conversation rather than through probing. Neutral subjects such as sports or hobbies may be the topics of choice. A subject to avoid would be race or racial issues. Religious topics should also be avoided. Religion tends to be a personal issue with African Americans but an impersonal issue with many others. Do not attempt to engage in friendly conversation with African Americans by mentioning gospel music because gospel music is so much a part of the religious experience that many African Americans do not separate it from their religion.

Racial themes should be avoided in friendly conversation mainly because of the volatile nature of the subject in society. If an outsider brings up a racial topic with an African American, for example, the African American at best may view it as an apology for America's dismal history of race relations; at worst he or she may view it as racism in the personal encounter.

The social worker engaging in friendly conversation with an ethnic minority person might consider the introduction of a personal problem touching lightly on an intimacy issue such as "I had trouble with my back last night." Self-disclosure on personal topics can result in sympathetic responses that lead to self-disclosure on the part of the other. Research suggests that social workers who wish for self-disclosure from the person being interviewed might self-disclose first to demonstrate the acceptance of self-disclosure and to model self-disclosure (Jourard & Jaffee, 1970).

As an avenue for the development of the working relationship, friendly conversation has long been ignored by professional helpers. Attention to the development of friendly conversational skills is an integral part of the ethnographic interviewing process. The social worker striving to become culturally competent should become skilled in the art of friendly conversation.

EXERCISES

The following exercises will help enhance your understanding of friendly conversation.

Exercise 1

Observe two persons engaged in friendly conversation. Write a short process of the communication interchange. Analyze the process using Spradley's model as a guide for your discussion.

Exercise 2

What do you think of the importance of developing the art of friendly conversation? Why is this skill an art rather than a science?

REFERENCES

Abad, V., Ramos, J., & Boyce, E. (1974). A model for delivery of mental health services to Spanish-speaking minorities. *American Journal of Orthopsychiatry, 44*(4), 584–595.

Benjamin, Alfred. (1974). *The helping interview*. New York: Houghton Mifflin.

Brammer, Lawrence M. (1973). *The helping relationship: Process and skills*. Englewood Cliffs, NJ: Prentice-Hall.

Gibbs, Jewell Taylor. (1985). Treatment relationships with black clients: Interpersonal vs. instrumental strategies. In Carel B. Germain (Ed.), *Advances in clinical social work practice* (pp. 184–196). Silver Springs, MD: National Association of Social Workers.

Jourard, Sidney M., & Jaffee, Peggy E. (1970). Influence of an interviewer's self-disclosure on the self-disclosing behavior of interviewees. *Journal of Counseling Psychology, 17*(3), 252–257.

Kadushin, Alfred. (1972). *The social work interview*. New York: Columbia University Press.

Perlman, Helen Harris. (1972). *Relationship: The heart of helping people*. Chicago: The University of Chicago Press.

Solomon, Barbara. (1976). *Black empowerment: Social work in oppressed communities*. New York: Columbia University Press.

———. (1985). The roundtable. In Sylvia Sims Gray, Ann Hartman, & Ellen S. Saalberg (Eds.), *Empowering the black family* (p. 73). Ann Arbor, MI: National Child Welfare Training Center, University of Michigan School of Social Work.

Spradley, James P. (1979). *The ethnographic interview*. New York: Holt, Rinehart, & Winston.

Vontress, Clemmont E. (1971). Racial differences: Impediments to rapport. *Journal of Counseling Psychology, 18*(1), 7–13.

7

SETTING THE STAGE FOR THE ETHNOGRAPHIC INTERVIEW

The most important experience of others takes place in face to face encounters; it is the exchange of gifts we call civility.
—*JOHN MURRAY CUDDIHY, 1974*

The interview can be seen as an event on a stage where actors play out roles as demanded by a script. The stage set contains props to assist in the unfolding of the story. We like the analogy of the stage to frame the ethnographic interview. The interview is a cultural event in which the dyad attempts to create a culture that each person learns and uses to form a working relationship.

An interview consists of three definable areas: the beginning, the middle, and the end (Johnson, 1986). The beginning of the ethnographic model of interviewing is marked by engagement in friendly conversation and communication that explains the process to be followed and the roles of the social worker and the person being interviewed. These activities set the stage for the middle phase of the conversation. In subsequent chapters the middle and ending activities will be presented.

FRIENDLY CONVERSATION

The first subcategory of the beginning phase is engagement in friendly conversation. Its content will depend on the specific circumstances of the opening comments. When the curtain opens, words are said or actions carried out that serve to get the interaction started. The content can be introduced by any party to the interaction. The parties may share food, discuss current events, talk about the weather, or comment on a current news item. If the contact is in the home of the interviewee, the social worker may choose to make friendly inquiries about amenities such as pictures on display. Such amenities are props that embellish the stage set on which the interview will be enacted.

As we noted in an earlier chapter, friendly conversation is an art and should be entered into with comfort and ease as it not only sets the tone for the conversation, but also enables the parties to hear each other's voices in a nonthreatening situation. Friendly conversation also presents the social worker as an interested and accepting human being, a condition vital to the formation of the helping relationship in cross-cultural situations.

THE MODEL EXPLANATIONS

After the friendly conversation phase, the social worker will begin to explain the ethnographic focus and its purpose, the process that will unfold, and the roles of each person in the ethnographic interview (Werner & Schoepfle, 1987, 303). Exactly when a social worker will shift to a discussion of these areas depends on his or her judgment or on the person's shift into questions. If the person makes the shift, the social worker should follow, as it means the person wishes to move forward in the interview.

Precisely how these areas are introduced may differ, but the content must be covered in every interview, and the person must agree to the ethnographic model. At times the areas of information will overlap one another. Social workers who are skilled at ethnographic interviewing will be comfortable explaining its purpose and process, but those who are less proficient in using the ethnographic model will find this phase awkward. As with all communication skills, frequent use will bring improvement. Most social workers can explain the purpose and work of the agency to people with no difficulty but are less accustomed to explaining the roles of the parties and the process of the interview.

The social worker should explain the explicit purpose and give ethnographic explanations, according to Spradley (1979, 59), because many clients are unfamiliar with this form of interviewing. The client's role as teacher or cultural guide must be explained before the social worker asks for the client's permission to play it. Spradley (59–60) states the following:

Explicit Purpose

When an ethnographer and informant meet together for an interview, both realize that the talking is supposed to go somewhere. The informant only has a hazy idea about this purpose; the ethnographer must make it clear. Each time they meet it is necessary to remind the informant where the interview is to go. Because ethnographic interviews involve purpose and direction, they will tend to be more formal than friendly conversation. Without being authoritarian, the ethnographer gradually takes more control of the talking, directing it in those channels that lead to discovering the cultural knowledge of the informant.

Ethnographic Explanations

From the first encounter until the last interview, the ethnographer must repeatedly offer explanations to the informant. While learning an informant's culture, the informant also learns something—to become a teacher. Explanations of the following areas facilitate this process:

- *Recording explanations.* These include all statements about writing things down and reasons for tape recording the interviews. "I'd like to write some of this down," or "I'd like to tape record our interview so I can go over it later, would that be OK?"
- *Native language explanations.* Since the goal of ethnography is to describe a culture in its own terms, the ethnographer seeks to encourage informants to speak in the same way they would talk to others *in their cultural scene*. These explanations remind informants *not* to use their translation competence. They take several forms and must be repeated frequently in the interview. A typical native language explanation might be, "If you were talking to a customer, what would you say."
- *Question explanations.* The ethnographer's main tool for discovering another person's cultural knowledge is the ethnographic question. Since there are many different kinds, it is important to explain them as they are used. "I want to ask you a different type of question," may suffice in some cases. At other times it is necessary to provide a more detailed explanation of what is going on.

The following beginning communications illustrate how different social workers focus on the stage-setting phase of the ethnographic interview.

1

I said that the ethnographic interview was a process for me to learn as much as I could about how he viewed aspects of his world. I said different words mean different things to different people due to our different life experiences. I would ask him to elaborate on these words in the interview. He said fine.

2

The interview I am going to conduct is a way of really having a good understanding of what your worldview is like. That is real important to me as we begin to work together. I will get a feel for your big picture of life. It is like you will be my guide, like you will be my teacher, because you are the expert on your world. You know what it is like for you, and I am coming into that world fresh and new, and I want to be sure that I can stand next to you while we are in this process together.

So what I'll do is ask you some pretty large questions and then I'll follow them and ask you about words and phrases that you use, but I'll need some clarification so I know what you mean by them. Are there any things you want to tell me about to get us started?

3

My approach to this interview was very straightforward. I told her I was interested in how she and her friends lived as homeless people. I told her she could teach me a lot. I said that she could back out of any agreement she would make at any time.

4

The client and I sat down together and I explained how the ethnographic interview worked and the things I would be doing such as writing down what was said, asking her questions, and I told her what the purpose was. The client understood and agreed to have the interview.

5

The purpose of the interview is that I will gain some knowledge of the client's culture that is unknown to me. So, in actuality, you are placed in the role of teacher and I am a learner.

6

Mr. O was very friendly and cooperative. I asked him if I could record the interview and he agreed. I explained that I found it helpful in my work with people to learn about the cultural backgrounds of people and that I would like to learn his views on his cultural background and the views of people he knew. I told him he was under no obligation to do this. Mr. O said he was flattered that I thought I could learn something from him and he would like to help me out as he might learn something also. I also explained to Mr. O that all the information he was willing to share with me about his lifestyle and his cultural group would be very helpful to me in helping him with his problems.

7

This interview may be a bit different from others you have had with social workers. They usually ask you a lot of questions. In this case, I'd like you to be a teacher and teach me about people with whom you share experiences and activities. So you will be the expert, not me. One area I am interested in learning about is the school you and your friends attend. I don't know much about how your group experiences school. So in other words, I want to know about the people around you. If these areas are all right with you, I will be writing down what you say, particularly the words you use. I may even go back to your words to explore with you how they are used with your group. This may seem stupid to you but words are used differently by many people and I want to be sure I know how they are used in your group.

EXPRESSING IGNORANCE

An aspect of the ethnographic stage-setting phase is the social worker's expression of ignorance about the culture of the person. According to Spradley (1979, 57), the expression of ignorance is an important part of engaging in friendly conversation. It encourages the other party to talk and continue talking. When people suggest they know all about the topic or subject under discussion, they convey a message of impending boredom and disinterest.

In the beginning phase of the ethnographic interview the social worker knows nothing about the cultural imperatives of the person. A statement conveying this message is appropriate very early in the interview, opening all avenues of the person's worldview for exploration. Sometimes when a social worker states ignorance, the person will question the statement. The social worker then has an opportunity to individualize the person and his or her perspective against any knowledge that is gained from other sources about the person or the cultural group the person represents.

Even during the ethnographic interview, expressions of ignorance are used to reinforce the person's cultural guide role as topics like family roles and religious beliefs are raised. If the social worker implies or states knowledge in the area, then the person will question the social worker's motive for asking. When this occurs in the interview, the social worker has departed from the ethnographic model.

When the social worker expresses ignorance in the stage-setting phase of the ethnographic interview, all information offered by the person is new. A frame is set for the person's future disclosures. Expressing ignorance is demonstrated in the following case.

The Case of Mr. C

The client was a black man, just out of prison, who was assigned to a white male social worker for treatment. The first two sessions were nonproductive in the social worker's opinion as the client was guarded and aloof. The client answered all the social worker's questions but did not elaborate. The client frequently stated he did not know information of a social history nature.

The social worker did not think they would be able to continue much longer although the client kept appointments and was on time. The social worker believed that the client might do better in a therapy group or with another social worker of the same race.

In the next interview the social worker was feeling a bit frustrated in getting the client to talk. He said to the client, "You know, I know quite a bit about psychology and I have been successful as a social worker. But I just don't understand you. You have been in prison; you are black; and you are in a strange place like this office and you are talking to a person you do not know and may not want to know. Maybe you should be the one who helps me understand you."

The client said, "What would you like to know about me? I am black; I have been in prison, and there are a lot more like me there and there will be many more due to the way society looks on black men."

From an ethnographic perspective, it was now time for the social worker to enter into the middle phase of the interview. The response of the client was directly related to the social worker's expression of ignorance about vital elements of his life. if the social worker were to be of help, an understanding of the worldview of a black man recently released from

Prison would include how he responded culturally to the prison and to the society that sent him there.

Every interview that occurs within a helping context begins with apprehension and varied expectations, stated or nonstated, on the part of the interviewee. Marziali (1988, 23) notes that at the first meeting the person and the social worker must adapt quickly to a situation that calls for the social worker to demonstrate how the process of help will be carried out between them. The stage-setting phase of the ethnographic interview addresses apprehension through open discussion of the purpose and process of the ethnographic interview. The stage-setting phase gives the social worker an opportunity not only to get the person to talk, but also to show interest and a nonjudgmental manner.

Explanation of purpose and process is vital in this phase but can be repeated throughout the ethnographic interview. Repeated explanations of purpose and process can reinforce the person's valuable contribution to the social worker's understanding of the person in culture configuration.

Successful completion of the beginning phase of the ethnographic interviewing model leaves both the social worker and the person knowing what to expect from each other. Each knows the goal is to discover the way cultural imperatives work for the person to be helped in the language of the person. By openly agreeing to the purpose and process, the person accepts the role of cultural guide and teacher and has a heightened sense of cooperation. The social worker is now at the point of beginning the gathering of ethnographic data. Asking a prepared or negotiated global question moves the social worker to the threshold of the other's cultural world.

EXERCISE

In this exercise you will practice the process skills for stage setting the interview.

1. Select a partner who will act as the person and prepare a simulated ethnographic interview using the stage-setting skills presented in this chapter.
2. Videotape the simulated interview.
3. Ask your partner to critique your interview.
4. Write a self-evaluation of your skills in stage setting the interview.
5. Reverse your roles.

REFERENCES

Cuddihy, J. M. (1974). *The ordeal of civility.* New York: Basic Books.

Johnson, Louise A. (1986). *Social work practice.* Boston: Allyn & Bacon.

Marziali, Elsa. (1988). The first session: An interpersonal encounter. *Social Casework,* 6(1), 23–27.

Spradley, James P. (1979). *The ethnographic interview.* New York: Holt, Rinehart, & Winston.

Werner, Oswald, & Schoepfle, G. Mark. (1987). *Systematic fieldwork: Foundations of ethnography and interviewing.* Beverly Hills, CA: Sage.

8

GLOBAL QUESTIONS

*There are, it may be, so many kinds of
language in the world, and none
of them is without significance.*

*Therefore, if I do not know the meaning
of the language, I shall be a foreigner to
him who speaks, and he who speaks will be a
foreigner to me.—1 COR., 14: 10, 11*

PRIOR TO THE CONTACT

The helping interview commonly begins with the eliciting of information
that develops a social history related to the presenting problem. Many social
workers use prepared questionnaires to guide and focus the interview content in the study phase of the helping process. Some social workers forgo the
formal questionnaire and ask a series of questions that serve as an informal
framework for gathering the social history information. This is a less structured approach to social history taking. However it is gathered, the obtained
information is used to formulate an assessment and treatment plan.

The ethnographic interview model offers an alternative to the traditional
process of information gathering in that it does not require taking a social
history. Rather than look at the life of the person, the social worker may think
about the person prior to the interview and write down any personal or
professionally puzzling questions the answers to which would lead them
into the cultural context of the person's life.

For example, say a social worker has been assigned the case of a woman
whose children were removed to a detention center after being found at
home alone. The woman works as a club dancer and is Native American.

Following an ethnographic framework, the social worker would formulate global questions reflecting initially puzzling thoughts about aspects of the woman's cultural frame. The list might include global questions such as the following:

1. What kind of club does she work in?
2. How does one find employment as a club dancer?
3. How many Native American women dance in clubs?
4. How do people react to her dancing?

Another social worker was assigned to assist a fifteen-year-old African American girl who had approached the school principal to ask how she could learn more about "problems kids have." The social worker had worked with African American adults but not with African American adolescents and had only read about the high drop-out rates and drug usage among the adolescents in the school. After attending an in-service training session where the ethnographic approach to interviewing was presented, the social worker decided to draw on an admitted lack of knowledge about African American adolescents and try this approach with the new client. The following global questions were formulated prior to the interview:

1. How do the young woman and her friends describe the school?
2. What occurs when she is with her friends outside of school?
3. How did she happen to talk to the principal of the school?

A list of global questions prepared prior to the ethnographic interview may seem irrelevant to problem solving, but to the social worker they could create communication barriers if left unanswered. The thinking in this area is that every social worker raises internal questions about some aspect of a case situation, and if the questions are not brought out in the interview, they will remain as barriers to listening and the overall helping process. Formulating initial reactions into global questions provides the social worker an opportunity to address these initial concerns within a learning context.

This phase of the ethnographic interview model is akin to Shulman's (1979, 14) *preparatory empathy* stage of the interactional process. This pre-contact stage of the helping process allows the social worker to tune in to the person by thinking about the person and the presenting problem. As the social worker begins to develop sensitivity to what the person may be communicating in the interview, he or she moves toward a state of empathy.

Empathy is the ability to get in touch with the feelings and concerns that the person may bring to the encounter. The social worker considers what feelings the person may have about requesting help. These feelings may include caution, fear, elation, depression, or suspicion. They may be concerns related to indecisiveness about getting help, puzzlement about what getting help is, and fears of what will happen in the process of being helped. The ethnic minority person may have questions about the agency and whether it can be of help or is even interested in giving help. Minority clients may also have questions about the ethnicity, culture, and race of the social worker.

The ethnographic approach adds another dimension to the preparatory stage. The assumption is made that the social worker may have either formal, informal, or no experience with persons they encounter. Like education, past experience may provide knowledge but cannot be used as a blueprint for present encounters with individual ethnic minority persons. The uniqueness of the individual prevails. To view the ethnic minority person as similar to all others of his or her cultural group is stereotyping. The social worker must see the uniqueness of the person as both similar and vastly different from past familiar situations without judging at first similar or different in what respects. Solomon (1985, 11) cautions social workers to consider "it takes two measures to describe a population: a central tendency and a measure of dispersion. It is essential to know the variations as it is to know what the central tendencies are." Central tendency thrusts are mitigated by remembering that each case is different from all other cases no matter how alike they may seem to be. The social worker must view the person as a universe of one and not as a standard example of a category.

The social worker should remember that the objective of the ethnographic approach is to learn about cultural behavior, values, language, and worldviews of the person who is representative of the cultural group, and to use this information in a process that results in treatment planning and intervention strategies that are congruent with the cultural demands of the person.

With this objective in mind, the social worker in this step of the ethnographic interviewing model may formulate global questions based not only on general areas of learning about the cultural group, but also on the social worker's initial reactions and questions that, if answered, would clarify issues related to providing services to the person. In this step, concentration is on the development of inquiries that, when responded to, will give the social worker a view of the person's world from the person's perspective.

The ethnographic interview is essentially a process of discovery. To gain understanding of the person and the situation, the social worker must obtain information that reflects the person's worldview. The particular world consists of cultural scenes. Ethnic minority people who seek help do not turn away from their cultural scenes when relating to the helping process. On the contrary, they may cling to their own cultural set for support in an unfamiliar culture.

At the same time, the ethnic minority person is part of a larger society, and the existing problems may actually result from the tug-of-war between the two cultural identities. It is important for the social worker to consider the current state of a person's cultural identity and development, for assessment purposes, early in the helping encounter. Lum (1986, 5) asserts:

> Minority social work starts by determining whether ethnic minority and cultural elements are useful functioning forces or barriers to meaningful living. In order to make a determination, the social worker should find out about family systems and other important ethnic information areas. The worker should ask the client to share meaningful minority perspectives on the problem.

As social workers begin to consider helping members of minority cultural groups, they should formulate questions about things that puzzle them professionally because culture is an element in the creation, definition, and solution of problems.

The presenting problem may have to do with unmet economic, medical, or educational needs, or it may be related to psychological, social, or physical stress. Presenting problems usually involve questions or situations that pose uncertainty, perplexity, or other difficulty. Most people are able to resolve their problems through personal or social resources. Others find no formal or informal culturally related sources of help and turn to society's institutions for assistance in meeting their needs.

Whatever the area of the presenting problem, the social worker has to view it in conjunction with the cultural world of the person who has or is said to have the problem. The extent of the problem must be ascertained within the cultural context of the person.

Most people are a part of several cultural scenes. They may be parents, members of formal or informal groups, employees, church members, and so on. Social workers rarely know much about the ramifications of each cultural scene for the individual, yet such knowledge may be very helpful in designing helping procedures to achieve problem solutions. This knowledge is best obtained from the individuals themselves.

Say, for example, an African American family presents problems related to the failure of the sixteen-year-old son in high school. The father is employed as a construction worker. The mother is unemployed. In this case situation, several cultural scenes seem present: the culture of the family, the culture of the son's school, the cultural implications of the parental roles, and perhaps even the culture of the father's workplace and the interplay between the family culture and the dominant culture of the external environment.

The social worker using an ethnographic approach would attempt to gather information from the perspective of the family as a unit and as individuals acting in a variety of cultural scenes. This would assist in formulating with the family members an intervention plan congruent with their cultural scenes. The approach might even point to areas in which, unbeknownst to family members, various cultural scenes are in conflict.

In formulating the global questions, social workers may seek assistance from peers or supervisors who have personal or professional experience. In this way the social worker can begin the learning process prior to becoming a learner in the actual cross-cultural helping situation. Such rehearsal may make the social worker more comfortable in the role of learner, which is the role he or she will take in the actual interview.

WITHIN THE ETHNOGRAPHIC INTERVIEW

Two general areas of global questions can be formulated during the interview:

1. Questions regarding the person's perception of how the community works along any dimension such as definition of problems, group role norms, important rituals and rites, how people get help and from whom, and accepted ways of problem resolution.
2. Questions regarding how the person relates to community cultural values, norms of behavior, and worldviews.

The questions may range in depth and breath depending on the nature of the presenting problem. A problem in the area of health may lend itself to global questions relating to definitions of illness, whom one consults and why when one is ill, and solutions accepted by the community and the person. A problem with relationships may require global questions about the gender roles of adults and children, how disputes are resolved, at what point a family's difficulties become public, and so forth.

Kleinman, Eisenberg, and Good (1978) offer a framework for formulating global questions in the interview. It distinguishes global questions as either personal or community related. For example, the social worker who wishes to focus on the personal might ask the following:

1. How did the problem happen?
2. What brought the problem on?
3. Why are you having the problem now?
4. How would *you* treat the problem?
5. What does the problem mean to you in terms of your daily life?

A focus on the community might result in global questions such as the following:

1. How does your community think such problems occur?
2. What reasons are given in your community for such problems occurring?
3. In your community why would people think they would have the problem?
4. How would others treat the problem?
5. What would this problem mean to others in terms of their daily life?

Answers to these questions would give the social worker notions that clients have about cultural-based problems (Kleinman, 1988a, 121).

Global questions can be formulated in the interview using the concepts of space, time, and actors. Examples of space-related global questions:

1. Can you take me through the neighborhood?
2. Pretend I am blindfolded. Explain the location in detail.
3. Describe the clubroom to me.

Examples of time-related global questions:

1. What are the daily activities of the people?
2. What do they do for recreation?

Examples of actor-related global questions:

1. Who are the people in this space?
2. What are their titles?
3. What do they do?

Global questions should not ask the person to evaluate the space, the time, or the actors. Evaluations are personal matters, and individuals may not trust the social worker enough to talk about how they evaluate their cultural environment. Evaluations may surface, however, as a person talks in response to global questions.

The global question should be in an open-ended format that keeps the person interested and talking. Avoid closed-ended global questions. The length of the global question is important. As a general rule, the longer the global question, the more detailed the answer will be. For example:

1. (Poor) What happens during the church service?
2. (Better) Church services generally follow a form of prayers and singing. Tell me about the specific process of service at your church.

Global questions are general, open-ended questions about some aspect of the interviewee's life, something that is personally or professionally puzzling to the social worker yet potentially salient to the presenting problem. The purpose of the global question in the ethnographic model is to generate a conversation, not to take a social history or explore the presenting problem. The global question should not focus on the person's motives or personal experiences.

When developing global questions, the social worker has to keep in mind that the wanted information derives from the person's cultural, not psychological, frame. Such global questions as "How do you feel about your father?" direct attention to self, not to the environment within which the person and father exist. To avoid a strict focus on the psychological, the social worker should not use the word "you" when formulating global questions. Collective words or phrases such as "people in the community," "others in the community," "members of the church," and "friends of yours" are more appropriate.

In the ethnographic model the objective is to receive information that frames the person's perception of norms, values, and behaviors of the cultural world. The social worker wants to learn about the person's world as viewed by the person. Therefore the global questions should direct the person telling the narrative to explore that cultural world. The social worker first wants to learn how that world operates, not how the person feels about that world.

Global questions may also depend on the social worker's understanding of the culture and the function of the helping agency itself. Agency rules and policies may dictate what information-gathering procedures can be used for the interview. Some agencies need specific information about the presenting problem for quick determination of child placement for those who are at risk physically or emotionally. In such situations the social worker may not be able to use the ethnographic interview model in the beginning phase of the helping process. After the immediate decisions are made and the case is ongoing, the social worker may have an opportunity to learn about the client's cultural world. Perhaps that information will lead to reunification of the family.

NEGOTIATED OPTIONS

Some social workers experienced in the ethnographic interviewing model choose to incorporate the formulation of questions into the interview, entering with a list of global questions and saying to the cultural guide, "I have made up this list of questions that indicate areas of my interests. What do you think of them?" Through this process, the social worker and the person negotiate the appropriateness of the global questions for inquiry and learning. Thus the social worker demonstrates respect for the person's input and enables the person to have an investment in the helping process.

This process also has the advantage of ascertaining the person's depth of cultural knowledge. While every person is a repository of cultural knowledge that accrues to a group over time, and while this knowledge is accessible through language, people think of themselves as experts not on their total culture but only on certain aspects of it. Some persons may be uninformed as to rites and religious customs, for example, but knowledgeable about the roles of family members and help-seeking behaviors of the cultural group.

The social worker may need a period of time to ascertain the extent of the person's cultural identification and willingness to share cultural information with a stranger. The social worker may want to discover the extent of the person's cultural involvement and the extent to which the person is involved in the cultural scenes. The stage is set for a negotiation process that can itself be therapeutic as the person is asked to reflect on his or her knowledge of self in the culture and to decide what areas of that knowledge can be shared with an outsider.

Deciding on global questions prior to or even during the ethnographic interview can be the most difficult task for the beginning ethnographic interviewer, who may lack the general cultural knowledge necessary to come up with appropriate global questions. Some can think only of social history questions such as "When did you come to this country?" or "What are the ages of the children?" Other social workers are not certain that their formulated global questions will be relevant or pertinent to the person's reason for seeking help. The inexperienced ethnographic interviewer may have trepidation as to whether the person will be able or willing to answer the global question. Some social workers have difficulty formulating global questions because they have not grasped the theoretical framework for ethnographic interviewing and are unable to make the paradigm shift from other models of interviewing to the ethnographic model.

In such instances, the social worker may not formulate global questions prior to the ethnographic interview but, according to Werner and Schoepfle (1987, 319–320), may inform the person of their areas of cultural interest (e.g., rites, help-seeking behaviors, methods of child rearing and discipline, and language patterns). The person is asked to comment on the mentioned areas, having the freedom to instruct the social worker about which cultural areas are acceptable for inquiry.

An exchange of views and information ensues between the social worker and the person. Clarification from each party in the encounter occurs. Negotiating the global questions results in questions that each has a stake in answering, as each has a participatory relationship with the other; that is, each party's views and thoughts are taken seriously by the other. Answers to the global questions are "at least in principle" separate tasks (Werner &

Schoepfle, 1987, 322). The social worker must keep the focus on agreed-upon areas of interest, not on obtaining answers. Through this approach, topics of interest to the social worker as learner and the person as teacher may lead to more culturally reliable information when separated from obtaining information about the areas of interest to both.

Imagination and creativity on the part of the social worker can result in other options for arriving at appropriate global questions for precontact formulation or for use during the ethnographic interview. The social worker working with children at a specific school may hang around with them on the playground or in the halls and listen for questions that they ask one another. The social worker may hear the children question one another on how to deal with certain teachers or how to relate to their parents. Important to this option for generating global questions is that the social worker first has to be an observer of the cultural scene. The scene has to be one in which the actors ask one another questions: children asking children, children asking parents, inmates asking inmates, or ethnic minority persons asking ethnic minority persons. The social worker should note the questions that the insiders ask one another and incorporate these questions into their global areas of interest.

EXERCISES

Exercise 1

Use the following scenarios to practice writing global questions.

A

You have been assigned to supervise a sixteen-year-old Chinese American male on probation after he was found guilty of shoplifting at a department store. He is now on his way to your office.

1. Write three to five global questions that represent your thinking based on your understanding of the nature of global questions.
2. What personal barriers might you encounter in the interview with the probationer?
3. What strengths would you bring to the interview with the probationer?

B

Mrs. H is a twenty-nine-year-old woman from Central America. She has been in the city for two years. She states she suffers from *ataques* that came on very suddenly. A strange sensation like heat begins in her feet, travels up her body, and exits from her head, leaving her feeling like ice. In describing what causes the *ataques*, she mentions problems with her husband and bad dreams. Mrs. H suffers from these episodes whenever she has disagreements with any member of the family. One doctor prescribed Valium, but Mrs. H does not take them regularly as they upset her stomach. Another doctor thought to be good at treating *ataques* told her to separate from her husband, which she refuses to do.

1. Write three global questions related to the case.
2. Why are these three global questions important?

C

Discuss with your small group the value of the dialogue when negotiating with the minority person of color about areas of interest that could be used to agree upon global questions.

D

Discuss with your small group valid issues you might encounter when considering others' worldviews and values.

Exercise 2   A Cultural Case Study

To learn about the culture of another, first it is necessary to recognize what you already know or do not know and what you fear. This exercise is designed to reveal where you are in regard to a specific cultural group by interacting with a member of that group to learn the other's cultural perspective and then assessing the implications for this learning on your attitudes and knowledge about that culture. It will also provide an opportunity to practice interviewing skills based on an ethnographic framework.

1. Select a cultural group that you wish to learn about.
2. Write what you do know, the prejudices you may hold, and any other information that forms your present understanding of the cultural group.
3. Write three global questions that will serve to focus your inquiries about the cultural group in an interview with a cultural guide.
4. Select a cultural guide for your interview.
5. Conduct an interview using you global questions to elicit your cultural guide's knowledge of the cultural views of the cultural group.
6. Write a summary of the interview using the words of the cultural guide.
7. Write an evaluation of the impact of the interview process and the information learned on your attitudes, knowledge, and skill development as a culturally competent social worker.

Exercise 3   Cultural In-Group Perspectives

The culturally competent social worker is alerted to using central tendency knowledge in working with minorities of contrasting cultures. There may be wider contrasts within cultures than between cultures. This exercise will provide an opportunity for learning how persons within a cultural group may differ in their cultural views.

1. Select a cultural group that you know little or nothing about and write four global questions that reflect items that are personally or professionally puzzling to you.
2. Select two persons of the culture you chose in item 1, making sure they are of the same gender and as close as possible in age, education, and religion. Ask them to be your cultural guides.
3. Conduct an interview with each cultural guide using the same global questions.
4. After each interview, write a summary of the information obtained in the words of the cultural guide.
5. Compare the two summaries for contrasts, differences, and worldviews. Does your material support the idea of variations within a cultural group?

REFERENCES

Kleinman, Arthur. (1988). *The illness narrative: Suffering, healing, and the human condition.* New York: Basic Books.

Kleinman, Arthur, Eisenberg, Leon, & Good, Byron. (1978). Culture, illness and care: Clinical lessons from anthropologic and cross-cultural research. *Annals of Internal Medicine, 88,* 251–258.

Lum, Doman. (1986). *Social work practice and people of color.* Monterey, CA: Brooks/Cole.

Shulman, Lawrence. (1979). *The skills of helping.* Itasca, IL: F. E. Peacock.

Solomon, Barbara B. (1985). Assessment, service and black families. In Sylvia Sims Gray, Ann Hartman, & Ellen S. Saalberg (Eds.), *Empowering the black family* (pp. 10–20). Ann Arbor, MI: National Child Welfare Training Center, University of Michigan School of Social Work.

Werner, Oswald, & Schoepfle, G. Mark. (1987). *Systematic fieldwork: Foundations of ethnography and interviewing.* Beverly Hills, CA: Sage.

9

COVER TERMS

A word as symbol has different implications to
different persons. Only the study of individual's
associations to the word as symbol permits
understanding of what it signifies . . . it has its
own unique context and can only be understood
in that context.—BRUNO BETTELHEIM, 1983

Words are the bridges that facilitate communication between human beings. According to Rorty (1989, 73),

> All human beings carry about a set of words which they employ to justify their actions, their beliefs, and their lives. These are the words in which we formulate praise of our friends and contempt for our enemies, our long term projects, our deepest self-doubts and our highest hopes. They are the words in which we tell, sometimes prospectively, and sometimes retrospectively, the story of our lives. I shall call these words "final vocabularies."

A social worker may assume knowledge of the meanings of the words of the minority person and erroneously accept these meanings as personal convictions of truth. Assumptions are only prejudices or preconceived preferences or ideas and serve as barriers to understanding another person (Young-Bruehl, 1996). Culturally competent social workers are able to engage in a "restructuring of world view" which "requires a critical review of what the individuals believe is reality" (McPhatter, 1997, 264).

Cover terms are words that literally cover a range of ideas, meanings, objects, or relationships that make up the cultural guide's world. Cover terms are the social worker's guide to the cultural meanings that give structure to experience. A special effort must be made to learn the meanings of the cultural guide's cover terms. Failure to do so will result in not learning or understanding the perspectives of the cultural guide.

In ethnographic procedures, we are essentially concerned with culture and the connotations of words. In modern industrial society words are used to create boundaries for what is termed *civility*. Words constitute the major vehicle for social exchange, and social workers should know how words are used. Words can be used to conceal feelings and meanings that are central to the person's position in life. Word use is selective and words can be used differently by the same person in different social contexts. Words can hurt and oppress. Sampson (1993, 3) views words as "silent killers" used by those in power to define and control minorities. Words are constructed by dominant cultural groups to assure that minorities service the needs of those in power. Social workers need to be much more aware of how words constructed by dominant social forces define minority populations and may injure the self-identity of minority persons and be a factor in the presenting problem (Levin, 1993).

Social workers have not always been sensitive to their own use of words when engaged with persons of contrasting cultures. Social workers as well as clients may resort to jargonistic language to protect themselves from those who represent a contrast to them. The result of either effort is a widening of the cultural gap between the two. The tendency is to think language is no challenge if both speak the same language, but language itself is the challenge. Language can be used to open as well as close a culture to an outsider.

In their efforts to help and enable, social workers must move beyond the levels of language civility that can be fraught with dissimulation. Past negative evaluations often lead ethnic minority persons to keep their innermost thoughts and views secret. Hine (1994, 344) states, "The dynamics of dissemblance involved creating the appearance of disclosure, or openness about themselves and their feelings, while actually remaining an enigma." The social worker must accept and understand why words and language have been useful tools aiding in the survival of a group. It is only as members of a group have been able to develop language strategies with words that cover what they really think and feel, that they have been able to manage and survive in a hostile environment.

It is important to recognize that language can be used to negatively label and categorize minorities of color and "prescribe and limit the possibilities of the person to whom they are applied" (Green, 1982, 67). From the perspective of the minority person, words such as inferior, culturally deprived, nigger, and wetback, that define and negatively categorize, can be threatening and wounding to the self-esteem. Language can define social and legal definitions and identify cultural patterns. Language can contain words that have the force to inflict "narcissistic injuries" which "are special kinds of hurt that cut to the quick, that assail us where we live, that threaten our identity or our self-image, or our ego-ideal, or our self-esteem" (Levin, 1993, xiv). The profession of social work has a language that can "represent central concepts and reflect both attitudes and practices" (Tropp, 1974, 19). Social workers need to examine "three professional words (client, help, and worker) to more clearly symbolize just who we are and what we do and with whom" (21). For example, an examination of the word *help* could result in a change to the word *useful* as "people come to us for help, and we usually try to respond by being useful" Cecchin, Lane and Ray (1994, 38).

Social workers must look at language as a cultural product. Like social workers, clients have a specialized language that reflects their particular cultural orientation. This functions to define boundaries, to conceal inside information, and to preserve a sense of specialness and dignity among those familiar with the language.

Language is a means of communication and a tool for constructing reality. Green (1995) directs social workers to the significance of language in cross-cultural encounters. The task of the culturally responsive social worker is to acquire a common sense of another culture and to utilize that awareness in the delivery of social services. Language is a means to access that knowledge.

In this sense, language is a tool for constructing reality as well as for communicating about that reality. Language influences the way people perceive their world in the sense that it has an important role in molding a person's perception of reality. Assuming that we require language to think and that languages vary, it must be the case that speakers of different languages will perceive—and therefore construct reality—differently.

To learn someone's language is to enter into his or her world. Social workers must be able to look *into*, not at, the culture of the other. The culturally sensitive social worker must have a strong sense of what meanings are suggested by the language of the client. In general, social workers believe that by being empathic, caring, and accepting, they can learn the meaning of behavior and language. These concepts assume an ability to enter into the life of another without first learning the context and meanings of the words that person uses to describe behavior. The essence of cross-cultural practice is to comprehend what the person knows and how that knowledge is used in the person's everyday life. A central concern of the ethnographic interview is to understand the meaning and use of language rather than to demonstrate caring responses.

The social worker wishes to discover information because it not only has significance for the relationship, but also is central to the social worker's acquiring an awareness of the common sense of another culture and using that awareness in the delivery of services requested. Language is the means of access to that knowledge on which service to the individual is based.

WORDS AND PHRASES

After beginning the interview by asking a global question, the next step is listening for certain words and phrases that stand out in the cultural guide's response. Unfamiliar words and phrases will catch the ear because they are unfamiliar. But other words and phrases that seem to have special meaning to the cultural guide can be familiar ones. They may be jargon associated with a special group, but they may be ordinary words with a special reference that the social worker does not know.

Consider the following statement made by a social worker, in this case, assuming the role of cultural guide to his professional group:

> We see all kinds of youth. Just recently I worked with a young man who was very disturbed. I'd say he had severe low self-esteem. He hung out on the streets, would not go to school, and was a gang member. He was from a single-parent family, and his mother could not control him. I decided that was evidence of his being out of control and filed a court petition for placement out of the home.

This short piece of conversation contains a number of words and phrases that characterize the cultural world of a particular group of social workers. As a cultural guide, the social worker states that he sees "all kinds" of youth. How many kinds are there? What are the categories for classifying youth? Who decides what the categories are? How are these decisions made? The cultural guide states that the youth had "severe low self-esteem." What does that mean in terms of behavior? He is said to be "a gang member." How do youths get to be gang members? What do gang members do when they hang out? How do social workers file petitions?

From the cultural guide's words, another social worker could see that he is speaking from the perspective of a professional culture and uses the culture's jargon and technical vocabulary in ways that only professional group members would understand.

It is evident that how the cultural guide describes his experiences with clients is one way he and others construct the cultural workplace they share. That construction has profound implications for the safety of children, the experiences of adults within the legal process, and the long-term welfare of families. The cultural guide's words provide our most rapid access to the cultural group's private understandings shared among professional colleagues, and to the implicit and explicit values guiding their behavior.

Spradley (1979, 19) is of the opinion that people are essentially bilingual in that they can speak the language of their cultural group but also can translate that language into the language of the outsider. This ability is termed *translation competence* and is defined as "the ability to translate the meanings of one culture into a form that is appropriate for another culture." Everyone learns to translate their own culture when communicating with outsiders who speak a dialectic version of the same language. A social worker communicating with a school teacher will strive to translate the meaning of the social worker's professional language into the language of the teacher's professional culture. Interdisciplinary collaborative work is dependent on this two-way communication process. Success across disciplinary lines depends on the ability of the professionals involved to translate answers into the language of the one who is trying to learn.

People learn to shift back and forth among the languages of home, work, and school, and between men and women. We learn to speak one way to the minister, another way to friends. We automatically translate what we are asked into the language of the other who is trying to learn about it from us.

In social work practice such translation competence is not unknown. The person wishing help attempts to cooperate by supplying information that is culturally acceptable and congruent within the social worker's cultural set. A distortion of the person's world occurs, and if the social worker is not aware of this language dynamic, problems in the helping process are certain to occur.

THE PROCESS

As the cultural guide responds to the global questions at the beginning and throughout the interview, the social worker listens carefully for words and phrases that if explored, will lead more deeply into the cultural guide's cultural world and reveal a less generalized area of his or her social scene.

The social worker writes these words and phrases on paper as they are heard for later reference. They can be noted and reflected on immediately if the social worker is struck by a particular word or phrase, but it may be more important to let the cultural guide talk and to listen than to interrupt immediately.

The social worker can interrupt when it seems appropriate or where there is a natural break in the conversation. As the ethnographic interview progresses it is not uncommon for the cultural guide to catch on to the process and begin to identify his or her own cover terms. This is particularly true when the cultural guide has been given an open explanation of the process of the interview. Interruptions then become natural and are not experienced by the cultural guide as intrusive or a sign of insensitivity to the spoken words.

In answering a global question, the cultural guide uses language to convey something about the experiences of the group. A response to a global question might be as follows:

> My people are frustrated warriors. We have to take a lot of hard knocks from each other before we can understand other people. Other people have to get into our mentality.

In deciding what may be a cover term, the social worker should remember that cover terms are words or phrases that reveal some aspect of the cultural guide's experience. They are verbal markers and of high symbolic importance (Kaufman, 1986). They identify important thematic information in the cultural guide's background. Cover terms literally cover some range of culturally significant meanings. Their value to the social worker in discourse is as entrees to an unfamiliar world.

It is not difficult to identify words that seem to be jargon or argot. The social worker must also remember that words and phrases that sound familiar may also be viewed as cover terms. In the example given, the cover terms or phrases "frustrated warriors," "hard knocks," and "mentality," if explored, may reveal the meanings of the words from the perspective of the cultural guide.

By noting cover terms, the social worker reflects listening to what the cultural guide is relating and demonstrating that the words of the cultural guide are of tremendous importance to the process of helping. In this step of the ethnographic interviewing process, the choice of cover terms is not as random as it may seem. The social worker wishes to learn about certain areas of the cultural guide's social environment and will hear words and phrases through the medium of the presenting problem.

The ethnographic interview is not a process to show the culturally contrasting person that the social worker is interested in the culture as an area of curiosity. It is not an effort to reveal the psychic roots of the personal problem. It is a process that is reciprocal in context and leads to ethnographic insights that are important in rapport building and treatment of personal and social problems.

This can occur only when the social worker recognizes that the helping situation is characterized by the idea of contrasts in cultures between the social worker and the person being seen for help. Once this recognition takes place, the opportunity exists to make use of the cultural dimension (Hensen, 1983). The social worker can learn from others their ways of thinking about the culture they identify with on a daily basis. A tactical advantage develops out of the cultural contrasts.

By identifying cover terms the social worker begins the discovery process into the private world of cultural images. The private world is never so private as to conceal the powerful impact of the sustained social environment. How people deal with this through language may be an important key to assisting those who represent contrasting cultural imperatives to the social worker.

EXERCISE

This exercise will strengthen understanding of cover terms. Discuss the following:

1. The importance of the study of language for social work practice.
2. The importance of words and their usage from the perspective of the ethnographic interviewer.

REFERENCES

Cecchin, Gianfranco, Lane, Gerry, & Ray, Wendel A. (1994). *The Cybernetics of prejudices in the practice of psychotherapy*. London: Karnac.

Bettelheim, Bruno. (1983). *Freud and man's soul*. New York: Knopf.

Green, James W. (1995). *Cultural awareness in the human services*. (2nd ed.). Boston: Allyn and Bacon.

Hensen, James. (1983). *Cultural perspectives in family therapy*. Rockville, MD: Aspen Systems Corporation.

Hine, Darlene Clark. (1994). Rape and the inner lives of black women in the Middle West: Preliminary thoughts on the culture of dissemblance. In Ellen Carol DuBois and Vicki L. Ruiz (Eds.), *Unequal sisters: A multi-cultural reader in U.S. women's history* (pp. 324–347). New York: Routledge.

Kaufman, Sharon. (1986). *The ageless self*. New York: New American Library.

Levin, Jerome. (1993). *Slings and arrows: Narcissistic injury and its treatment*. Northvale, NJ: Jason Aronson.

McPhatter, A. R. (1997). Cultural competence in child welfare: What is it? How do we achieve it? What happens without it? *Child Welfare, LXXVI* (1), 255–278.

Rorty, R. (1989). *Contingency, irony and solidarity*. Cambridge, MA: Cambridge University Press.

Sampson, Edward. (1993). *Celebrating the other: A dialogic account of human nature*. Boulder, CO: Westview Press.

Spradley, James P. (1979). *The ethnographic interview*. New York: Holt, Rinehart & Winston.

Tropp, Emanuel. (1974). Three problematic concepts: Client, help and worker. *Social Casework, 55*(1), 19–29.

Young-Bruehl, Elisabeth. (1996). *The anatomy of prejudices*. Cambridge, MA: Harvard University Press.

10

DESCRIPTORS

Everyday life becomes a matter of role playing and
impression management. Can we go deeper?
—ANDREW CURRY, 1973

Social workers and other helping professionals are trained to elicit information of a personal nature from clients. The social worker keeps the client the center of attention through the use of questions. Questions are asked for many purposes in social work practice. They can be used to help a person tell a story or narrative, to help build a relationship, to explore options to treatment, to gather data related to a specific problem or complaint, to encourage people to consider other points of view.

During ethnographic interviewing, social workers ask questions designed to lead them into the cultural world of the other person. This is not to say that the social worker who uses ethnographic interviewing techniques is not interested in the individual. The individual is approached through learning related to the cultural variable contained in his or her social environment. This individual is only a reflection of meaningful cultural imperatives.

For example, a question geared to obtaining personal information might be "How did you relate to your teachers?" This question is focused on the personal evaluation of the person through the use of the word "you." Asking a person a question with "you" as the reference point forces the person to become introspective and thus personal. While this information may be useful, the objective is not to obtain ethnographic information.

The ethnographic approach requests that the social worker gain cultural information about the person's world perspective. A general rule is that an ethnographic approach guides the social worker to proceed from the general to the specific. To learn about the person, the social worker must first learn about the cultural world of the person. Then the person's behaviors, thoughts, problems, struggles, and strengths take on a clearer meaning within the context of the person's life. This is an important aspect of two basic principles of social work—acceptance and respect.

Most social work literature on interviewing encourages the social worker to be aware of a variety of questions that can be asked in the interview. These questions depend on the purpose of the interview, but all are given so that the social worker can obtain information to be used in the process of help. Kadushin (1972, 149) states:

> The successive questions should act as a funnel, moving from the general to the specific aspects of the content being discussed. As discussion of one area is completed at the more specific end of the funnel, the new content area introduced for discussion should start with another general, open-ended question. The movement is from "Could you tell me what it is like for you to live on an AFDC budget?" to "What did you do about food for the children the last time you ran out of money before the next check was due?"

Kadushin's interviewing guideline is a typical one for social workers and illustrates an essential difference from the thrust of ethnographic interviewing.

If one were to use an ethnographic interviewing guideline, then the focus of the general open-ended question might be, "What do people on AFDC do when money runs out before the next check?" This question would elicit information about a person's views relative to knowledge of how others within that world of AFDC persons manage. These questions would be in response to the cover term "AFDC." The ethnographic interviewer would have heard the term AFDC and focus on obtaining the descriptive information related to it. This occurs when the social worker engages the person in responses to open-ended questions that may provide information about how a group of persons relates to the stress of no income. Obtaining descriptive information is based on hearing cover terms. Spradley refers to these open-ended questions to obtain descriptors as asking structural questions (Spradley 1979, 60). These questions enable the social worker to discover information about how the person organizes knowledge as well as to ascertaining the person's view on a particular cultural area. If the social worker has heard the word "groovy" used by the person, the ethnographic response to obtain descriptors might be, "How do people act when they are described as groovy?" Asking for use rather than "meaning and motives" and eliminating "probing why" and "what do you mean" questions is a principle to follow in ethnographic interviewing (Spradley, 81–82).

QUESTIONS APPROPRIATE FOR THE ETHNOGRAPHIC INTERVIEW

The central method of interviewing is the fine art of questioning (Garret, 1972, 47). Questions are more than a form of inquiry; they are technical procedures in constant use in a variety of forms. A question that is used to elicit a yes-or-no answer is generally an indication of poor technique and a lack of skill in interviewing. Such questions are known as direct questions and can be perceived as intrusions and cross-examination.

In ethnographic interviewing, the descriptive form of question is the form of inquiry most often used to gather cultural information. Descriptive question formation is a major skill to be learned by those human service professionals who wish to become culturally competent.

Werner and Schoepfle (1987) label one type of descriptive question grand tour and four subtypes as space, time, actor, and evaluation. Grand tour questions are "macroscopic" and "aim specifically at eliciting key terms (words or phrases) in the context of their use" (318). Each type can be understood by focus on the subtypes as follows:

Descriptive Questions

A. Grand Tour Questions

1. *Space questions.* The objective of global space questions is to learn about the physical setting of the cultural scene or territory of action or stage on which the action occurs (322).
2. *Time questions.* Since all cultural activity occurs in temporal sequence, time questions provide the sequence of activities for social relationships (328).
3. *Actor questions.* All cultural scenes are peopled by actors. It is important to learn who the people are in relation to jobs, relationships to each other, and titles (328).
4. *Evaluation questions.* These questions ask for evaluations of things or people and ought to be linked to factual questions. Evaluation questions of a global nature should not be used early in the interview process as they may be threatening to the cultural guide as they are

highly personal and the cultural guide may not have developed the trust necessary to reveal "how one feels" to a stranger (333).

Spradley (1979, 85–89) presents the five types of descriptive questions: global, miniglobal, example, experience, and native language and several sub types. These types and subtypes are illustrated by the following material.

A. Global Questions

Global questions encourage the cultural guide to talk at length. The interviewer receives a verbal description of some significant features of the cultural scene.

1. Typical sentence questions
2. Specific questions
3. Guided questions
4. Task-related questions

B. Miniglobal Questions

Miniglobal questions are identical to global questions but cover a smaller unit of experience.

1. Typical sentence questions
2. Specific questions
3. Guided questions
4. Task-related questions

C. Example Questions

These questions are very specific. They take a single act or event by the cultural guide or others and ask for an example.

D. Experience Questions

This type of question merely asks the cultural guide for any experiences they have had in a particular setting.

E. Native Language Questions

1. Direct language questions

The purpose of this type of question is to learn how the cultural guide would define a cover term.

2. Hypothetical questions

This type of question places the cultural in an interactive situation and asks the cultural guide to speak as if talking to a member of his or her cultural group.

3. Typical sentence questions

The typical sentence question asks the cultural guide to take a cover term and use it in a typical way.

Exemplars

A. Global Questions
For example, a social worker might ask an opening global question "I'm interested in how people in your neighborhood help each other." The cultural guide might respond:

> All the women in my neighborhood are called on to help people with kids and to care for the sick. We are not paid as no one has much money. It is just what you were expected to do for the community.

A social worker might respond with any form of the following:

1. Typical sentence question:
Would you describe what your friends think might cause the sickness they are called upon to help with?

2. Specific question:
What would be done to help a sick person?

3. Guided question:
Would you show me the neighborhood and tell me about the living conditions of the people who live there?

4. Task-related question:
Can you draw me a picture of your neighborhood?

B. Miniglobal Questions

1. Typical sentence question:
I am interested in hearing what you think is the cause of the last sickness that you helped out with.

2. Specific question:
Could you describe what occurs from the time one arrives at a sick person's home until one leaves?

3. Guided question:
Could you show me where you live?

4. Task-related question:
Would you draw me a picture of the typical room in a house in your neighborhood?

C. Example Question
Could you give me an example of what your friends do when they help others?

D. Experience Questions
You may have had some interesting experiences helping others. Can you tell me about them?

E. Native Language Questions
1. Direct language question:
   Among your friends, would most say "community"?
2. Hypothetical question:
   If you were sitting around a table with other women, what would you be saying to each other about helping others in the neighborhood?
3. Typical sentence question:
   What would be some of the sentences in which one might use the phrase "got no money"?

By asking for descriptors of a cover term, the social worker starts to collect blocks of information relative to certain aspects of the person's worldview. Green and Leigh (1989, 9) refer to descriptors "as blocks of descriptive information, systematically collected, used to build a composite portrait of selected cultural characteristics more or less shared by a set of clients." Such questions function to explore the person's cultural knowledge. By using these questions geared to obtain descriptive data of one cover term, the social worker's need to interpret the meaning of the social context of the word is nullified. The person supplies the meaning for the social worker. Green (1982, 79) refers to descriptive information as "attributes of cover terms."

In the process of the interview, the social worker may interrupt the person to obtain descriptive information related to a cover term. At times the social worker may wait for a natural pause in the conversation, but a question to elicit descriptors justifies a direct interruption in the person's conversation.

If the social worker has explained the process of the ethnographic interview during its opening phase, the person will perceive the interruption as natural and not as an impolite intrusion. The person will relate to the inquiry and give more information, which will move the content into more depth. This information becomes a descriptive block of material related to the cover term and is culturally relevant information. It explains to the outsider, the social worker, the insider's view of an aspect of the culture. The purpose of the ethnographic interview is to obtain information related to the cultural world of the person. This purpose should always be kept in mind.

Obtaining descriptors or descriptive data related to the cover term is the third process step in the ethnographic interviewing. Such descriptive information flows from the cultural guide in response to inquiries about the cover terms the cultural guide has used. For example, suppose the cultural guide, in describing the people at the school, uses the word "homeboy."

The social worker notes this word and decides to explore it further. The social worker should not assume that the understanding of homeboy is the same between them. Many social workers will give a nonverbal message such as an affirmative nod of the head, when actually they understand such words only through their own cultural set and usage, not through the cultural definition of the person being interviewed.

An example of an inquiry focused on obtaining descriptors would be the following:

1. How would a homeboy be described?
2. What does a person do to become a homeboy?

As the cultural guide responds to such open-ended questions, the social worker should write down the stated words. This material becomes part of the ethnographic summary.

Descriptors can be considered as blocks of descriptive information, systematically collected and used to build a composite portrait of selected cultural characteristics of a set of persons known as clients, or known as being important in the social environment of the person.

When considering the collection of descriptive information, the social worker can be guided by four areas:

1. The person's definition and understanding of an experience as a problem.
2. The language people use to describe a problem.
3. The indigenous strategies of problem resolution including the identity and procedures of indigenous healers and advisors.
4. The culturally based criteria of problem resolution.

It is to be noted that to obtain descriptors, the social worker must formulate questions in the interview and as the interview progresses. The social worker will have to listen actively to the cultural guide and follow closely the words spoken. Through active listening, the social worker will hear many cover terms and must decide which ones to pursue. If the social worker has shared the ethnographic procedures thoroughly with the cultural guide and the cultural guide has agreed to participate in the interview as a cultural guide, no problems should ensue. The social worker will receive an abundance of descriptive material.

Descriptors are simply characteristics of a cover term, and the social worker using an ethnographic frame for the interview seeks to explore the description of each. Another example of this process is as follows:

SOCIAL WORKER: You mentioned people being known as bad. In your community what would a bad person do to be described with that word?

(The social worker decides to explore the cover term "bad" and asks a descriptive question.)

CULTURAL GUIDE: Well, you would have to not follow the rules of your family. People call the family like mine an extended family. Even if you are not related you are related. Grandparents or elderly people in the community set the trends for how you acted. Grandmothers decided you had to go to church, which was a family gathering. You saw everyone. You ate dinner with them. When something went wrong, the reason was that you didn't go to church. So the next Sunday, you went to church. If you didn't, you were really bad. *(The cultural guide relates to the social worker's inquiry and explains, from an insider's perspective, the cultural context of the word "bad." In addition the cultural guide opens other culturally relevant areas for inquiry.)*

Social workers with limited or no experience in using the ethnographic frame of interviewing should write down, during the interview, cover terms and descriptors. After gaining some experience, most social workers will find that they are able to hear cover terms by actively listening and remembering descriptive material. They will not have to record fully the material heard in the interview as they will naturally think in an ethnographic mind-set during the interview and respond appropriately to the cultural guide.

Often the cultural guide will use a term or word or phrase numerous times in sections of the interview. If the social worker is actively listening, these cover terms will stand out in the interview. When this occurs, a clue is present that the term, word, or phrase has deeper importance that the cultural guide may not be aware of or may mention as a way of opening the linguistic door to the culture, if the social worker wishes to enter. At other times, repeated use of cover terms can be a test by the cultural guide to ascertain if the social worker is listening and really wishes to learn. Whatever the reason for the repeated verbalization, the social worker should explore the cultural ramifications of the word, term, or phrase.

Suppose that in a hypothetical ethnographic interview, the social worker hears and writes down words and phrases and identifies the following cover terms: stoned, muddleheaded person, cop a plea, and burned out. The social worker should not assume knowledge of what these words and phrases cover from the cultural guide's perspective. To do so would suggest that language has universal connotations. False assumptions will occur if the social worker fails to explore the cultural context of the cover terms. To focus on eliciting descriptive material, the social worker should form a question related directly to the cover term or phrase.

The following illustrates the range of questions that can be asked of the cultural guide:

1. May I interrupt for a moment? I wonder how a muddleheaded person would be described.
2. A moment ago I heard the words "burned out." What happens when a person in your group burns out?
3. How is a muddleheaded person different from any other person?
4. If I were to be described as stoned, what would I have to be doing?
5. What does one do to cop a plea?
6. What does the family do to handle a muddleheaded person?

The person's response will take the social worker further into the other cultural world. As the cultural guide continues to teach the social worker the cultural context of the cover terms and phrases, more descriptive material will emerge.

The following examples of communication exchange illustrate questions that will elicit descriptors. They reveal the probing, exploring nature of questions appropriate to leading the ethnographic interview into the social cultural environment of the cultural guide.

Example 1

CULTURAL GUIDE: Well let's say you tell your friend that you blew it and went to bed with this girl and he tells another friend and he tells your father. Now that just won't work out. You are supposed to tell your friend something and it stays right there. That's it. It doesn't go any further. Keeping a confidence is best.

SOCIAL WORKER: What happens in the community when a person breaks a promise?

CULTURAL GUIDE: Depends on who it is and on how severe it is. One guy told where some stolen goods were. If they find him, they would kill him. If you break a confidence and it's not important you might just get beat up. It also depends on how important you are to everyone. People that are just so-so, just run away. If you are high up on the list you die or they allow you to stay.

Example 2

CULTURAL GUIDE: A family in town is a mother, a father and some kids. The mother and father are caring, loving, and understanding.

SOCIAL WORKER: What kinds of things do mother and father do to be caring?

CULTURAL GUIDE: They would take care of you, talk to you about your problems, and help you to understand what you do.

Example 3

CULTURAL GUIDE: In my neighborhood, if you did something wrong, you got your ass kicked.

SOCIAL WORKER: I have an idea what getting your ass kicked means, but what happens in your neighborhood when kids get their ass kicked?

CULTURAL GUIDE: (*Laughs*) Well, I'll tell you but I want you to tell me if it is the same in your neighborhood. In my neighborhood it meant your father, mothers never kick ass, would hit you with his hands and fists. He wouldn't hit your ass. All the time he would be hitting you, he would be talking about how wrong you are and how you had better not do it again. (*Laughs*)

Example 4

CULTURAL GUIDE: I'm an expert on game playing. Like all guys I know but I am better than they are. I've had games played on me by women and some of them are really vicious.

SOCIAL WORKER: Describe some of the games.

CULTURAL GUIDE: One is that you have been in a relationship long enough to know she is hooked. The game starts. You cheat, you sneak out, you manipulate. Now one has got to be stronger than the other.

SOCIAL WORKER: Stronger?

CULTURAL GUIDE: Mental fortitude. It is a head thing. Sometimes women I know are stronger and move guys around because guys are so wishy-washy. Maybe some guys need to have someone to boss them around A lot of men think women play dirty tricks, so they play them first.

EXERCISES

The following exercises will assist in the understanding of descriptors.

Exercise 1

1. Discuss the major focus of the third step in the ethnographic interview model.
2. Discuss the reason for obtaining descriptors.

Exercise 2 A Case Communication Sample

The following excerpt is from an ethnographic interview with a twenty-five-year-old African American woman describing her childhood.

> Play out late, climb trees, sliding down the big hill on cardboard. My grandmother said all the girls should have been boys, we slid down more hills than they did. I was more assertive, you know, being around boys and my brother he was more timid than me. But it was fun. There was a lot of apple trees that we used to climb. Cousins would come around and we were real close. We always kept my grandmother busy. My great grandmother was tough too. She broke her hip and you would think she could not get around.
>
> But her cane used to do tricks, like turn around a corner and come and get you. She was very loving. Over the years they got more mellow but they were as set in their ways; they are from way back when about everything was separated including black and white. We think that there are some kinds of black people that are different from white people. Black people give too much, white people are power hungry. My people share with the family net. But some can get beside themselves which can happen.

1. Write three global descriptive questions related to space, time, and actors.
2. Write three global descriptive questions related to typical, specific, guided, and task-related areas.
3. Write three miniglobal questions related to typical, specific, guided, and task-related areas.
4. Write an example descriptive question.
5. Write an experience descriptive question.
6. Write native language descriptive questions related to direct language, hypothetical, and typical questions.

Exercise 3 Check Your Knowledge

Complete the following statements.

1. In the ethnographic interview model the cultural guide designation is given to the person interviewed when
   a. the social worker performs a service for the person.
   b. an open agreement is obtained for the person to be a teacher.
   c. a supervisor approves the person.
   d. the social worker decides the person has the motivation for help.
2. The center of attention of ethnographic interviewing is
   a. obtaining a diagnosis.
   b. the presenting problem.
   c. the family interaction patterns.
   d. the social environmental world of the group.

3. In ethnographic interviewing the interview movement is from

  a. facts to feelings.
  b. general to specific.
  c. specific to general.
  d. diagnosis to treatment.

  4. An essential skill to be mastered in the third phase of ethnographic interviewing is

  a. active listening.
  b. demonstration of empathy.
  c. unconditional warmth.
  d. awareness of self.

5. Cultural information is best obtained by

  a. a mental status examination.
  b. ethnographic interviewing.
  c. obtaining a social history.
  d. reading books related to the culture.

Exercise 4   Writing Global Questions

Practice writing global questions in response to the following cultural guide statements.

CULTURAL GUIDE: I am president of the block club.

SOCIAL WORKER:

CULTURAL GUIDE: Keepers of the fire all are around the neighborhood.

SOCIAL WORKER:

CULTURAL GUIDE: Those kids get in trouble all the time.

SOCIAL WORKER:

REFERENCES

Curry, Andrew. (1973). *Bringing forth forms*. Paradise, CA: Dustbooks.

Garrett, Annette Marie. (1972). *Interviewing: Its principles and methods*. Revised by Elinor P. Zaki and Margaret Mangold. New York: Family Association of America.

Green, James W. (1982). *Cultural awareness in the human services*. Englewood Cliffs, NJ: Prentice Hall.

Green, James W. & Leigh, James W. (1989). Teaching ethnographic interviewing methods to social service workers. *Practicing Anthropology, 11*(3), 8–10.

Kadushin, Alfred. (1972). *The social work interview*. New York: Columbia University Press.

Spradley, James P. (1979). *The ethnographic interview*. New York: Holt, Rinehart & Winston.

Werner, Oswald, & Schoepfle, G. Mark. (1987). *Systematic fieldwork: Foundations of ethnography and interviewing*. Beverly Hills, CA: Sage.

11

TERMINATING THE INTERVIEW

*One of the most important features of talking
is the opportunity it offers us to explore the
nature of describing being here for one
another.—ANDREW CURRY, 1973*

Termination of the ethnographic interview begins near the end of the fixed
time limit. The time limit ought to be set during the preethnographic section of the interview proper. The social worker indicates the time limit on
the interaction and expresses appreciation for the cultural guide's cooperation. If there is to be a subsequent contact, its time and place are negotiated.
If this is the find contact, the social worker says so and asks if the cultural
guide wishes to add anything further. If it seems appropriate, the social
worker may return to friendly conversation before departing the ethnographic interview.

Termination of the helping interview is given minimal attention in the
professional literature. As termination is considered an important aspect of
the ethnographic interview, culturally appropriate methods of termination
seem in order.

The question is this: how can the social worker discover these culturally
appropriate ways to terminate interviews? Within any given cultural group
there are procedures a social worker can follow to signal clearly that an
encounter is over. What are the appropriate means of termination of human
encounters? Are there significant words to use with contrasting populations?
Are there ritualistic forms that one can initiate and participate in? Perhaps
during the ethnographic interview process itself, the social worker can learn
from the cultural guide culturally acceptable ways of leaving others. As the
social worker is learning the behaviors of a contrasting culture from one of its

members, the cultural guide may spontaneously reveal important ethno-graphic data related to termination of encounters. Wick (1977, 12) states,

> Once the interview has nearly completed its course, workers should close the session without leaving the client up in the air, without a sense of conclusion. If the situation is one in which only one inter-view is scheduled, the client should be permitted final questions and given prescriptive or referral information that may be appropriate prior to terminating the session. On the other hand, if the interview is one in a series, in many instances last minute questions may be deferred to a later session.

Maple's (1985, 95) advice to social workers relative to termination of the interview is "either party can indicate that he or she feels that it is finished. As no topic is ever completely handled, you will seldom experience an ending as a totally finished piece of work." The plan of action should be mentioned, if one is called for, or the objective for meeting can be restated. Both parties may talk about the experience of being in the interview and give each other impressions of the interview. The social worker ought to keep in mind that every interview session has a beginning, a middle, and an end.

Kadushin (1972, 207) states that the purpose of the interview should always be kept in mind. The purpose will give direction to the content of the termination phase of the interview. One needs to set limits on the interview time related to the purpose of the interview, and the interview should end before the parties are emotionally tired.

Verbal reminders can help. The social worker may say, "I wish we had more time," or "Our time is almost up." Verbal reminders can be supported by nonverbal gestures such as shifting in the chair, folding papers, standing up, preparing to shake hands, or actually opening a door and saying good-bye. These gestures may be particularly appropriate when the person is reluctant to leave. Next steps should be discussed. A brief recap of the interview content will tend to consolidate it and point to the possible content of forthcoming interviews.

Like all interviewing skills, termination procedures are important for the social worker to master. In ethnographic interviewing, the social worker needs to incorporate culturally appropriate measures into the termination procedure. The next step in the ethnographic interviewing process should be made clear—writing the ethnographic summary, for example, or sharing this summary with the person. All of the stages should be mentioned first in the opening phase of the ethnographic interview so the cultural guide will know what to expect.

Consensus in the professional literature is that the power of termination usually lies with the social worker although the person also has the power to terminate the interview. When working within the ethnographic model, the social worker should always strive to maintain a relationship of mutuality.

During the termination phase of an ethnographic interview, the social worker can share with the cultural guide any written notes concerning cover terms and descriptive material. If the cultural guide reads them, some correction may become part of the termination process. If the cultural guide does not read the notes, plans may be made to do so at the beginning of the next contact. By volunteering to have the "learning" checked by the cultural guide, the social worker reinforces the person's role as teacher.

Each termination of each ethnographic interview will be different. This is as it should be because the interview process dynamic is ruled by the traits and characters of the participants. As in all professional encounters, the art of practice may take precedence over the suggested guidelines. The art is "how" the suggested guidelines are put into practice.

The following excerpts illustrate how some social workers have terminated ethnographic interviews.

A

The thirty-minute tape ran out. I thanked him for his help in teaching me about his culture. He asked me how did I think he could be of help to me. I said that I had noticed that he seemed to be knowledgeable about his way of life and a good person to talk to about information on his cultural group. He thanked me for giving him the opportunity to think about himself and now he has a few things to think about. We arose from our chairs and moved toward the door. He said he hoped I was going to get an "A" for learning and if I failed to learn anything it was my problem. We both laughed as he walked out of the door and down the hall.

B

Our time was up. When I mentioned this, he said "that old devil clock" and smiled. I had my papers on the desk and he wondered had I gotten all the answers I needed. I said that he could look them over and the ones he wanted to talk about more could be the focus of our next meeting. He said he was free now and could stay longer. I thanked him for wanting to stay and continue but I had another appointment and had to leave. He then reached for the papers with the global questions on them and read through the questions silently. He mentioned that there were two I had not asked and he would think about them and tell me about them the next time. I agreed and we said good-bye.

C

I said that there were more areas I wanted to learn about but our time was up. She said that we had a lot of time to get together as I was going to be her social worker. She had a lot more to teach. I said I appreciated her sharing her views on her life with me and she was a great cultural guide. She said she did not know about that but she tried to do her best to teach me what she knew about Chinese culture.

D

At this point I stopped the ethnographic interview as our agreed upon time was up. I thanked her for being a resource to me and mentioned that several resources were available for day care for the children and handed her some material regarding children's nutrition which she had requested when she phoned me yesterday. We agreed to meet in three days at the same time to continue our discussion.

E

At this point the tape clicked off. I asked her did she want to continue. She replied that she would think about the high school and perhaps tell me more about it at our next interview. I said I would like that and thanked her for being my cultural guide. I said she had shared a lot with me and that I had learned a great deal. . . . She was a good teacher. She said she hoped to be a teacher one day and this was her first chance to teach anybody anything.

F

We both looked at the clock and knew it was time to finish. She said this had been so interesting for her that she hated to stop. I thanked her and said I had learned a lot. She said she did too and wanted to talk to me some more. I agreed and we set up a time to get together again.

G

L was telling me about the religious ceremony of his tribe when he said that was enough for today. He wanted to tell me more so I would understand what his people went through and what gets them through it but he was a little shaky now. He wanted to be sure that I did not take up the life he had been talking about. I thanked him for sharing his ideas with me. I appreciated his agreeing to be my cultural guide. I mentioned he was a good teacher. He said he was willing to give me lessons any time.

H

I said that looks like all the time we have for now. Thank you for letting me record our conversation today. She said it was fun and that being Indian was very important to her and she wanted to talk about what people she knows are all about. We said good-bye after arranging for another meeting.

I

I said our time was up. Let's pick up where we left off the next time. Is there anything that you want me to know before we part? She said no and she would see me again. We then parted.

J

I hated to cut her off but our time was up. She was right in the middle of telling me about how mothers in the neighborhood shared baby-sitting arrangements. She said she felt that she had been lecturing me and generally social workers did not like people to lecture them. She added she hoped she had been helpful. I said she had and I appreciated her openness and candor. I added I would like to see her at the same time next week. She readily agreed to coming to her next class to teach.

REFERENCES

Curry, Andrew. (1973). *Bringing forth forms*. Paradise, CA: Dustbooks.

Kadushin, Alfred. (1972). *The social work interview*. New York: Columbia University Press.

Maple, Frank F. (1985). *Dynamic interviewing: An introduction to counseling*. Beverly Hills, CA: Sage.

Wick, Robert J. (1977). *Strategies and intervention techniques for the human services*. Philadelphia: Lippincott.

12

THE ETHNOGRAPHIC INTERVIEW SUMMARY

I'll talk to you all day long,
but don't interview me.
—LUCY ANN MELTON, 1980

The social worker should review the data recorded in the interview, paying attention to the cover terms and the descriptive information obtained for each one. Cover terms supported by descriptive information reveal elements of the culture. After a series of ethnographic interviews, summaries can be merged to give a comprehensive description of cultural elements learned from the client over time.

The ethnographic summary reflects directly the words of the cultural guide. The purpose of the ethnographic model of interviewing for cross-cultural helping encounters is not to determine the truth or accuracy of the person's report. The social worker does not have to be concerned with trusting the cultural guide; the social worker's concern is an open acceptance of the other's narrative. For this model, the narrative is the truth. The person is encouraged to tell the narrative, and the social worker gives up initial perceptions to gain a closer understanding of what the person wishes to convey. The social worker must listen to the narrative of the cultural guide. If the social worker does not, the cultural guide may experience a sense of being invisible similar to Ellison's (1952, 3) declaration, "When they approach me they see only my surroundings, themselves, or figments of their imagination—indeed, everything and anything except me."

The social worker does not interpret any of the information. The ethnographic summary might reveal the person's and community's definition of the problem, the cultural meanings and descriptions of a variety of cultural scenes, and the person's ability to use adaptive cultural mechanisms for problem solving.

The ethnographic interview summary might also reveal the cultural patterns of family relationships, help-seeking and child-rearing behaviors, and the norms and values attached thereto. The ethnographic interview as a totality contains the person's views on his or her culture and relationship to that culture. All of this is obtained through the language of the person who is part of the cultural group. For the social worker, the summary should reveal the aspects of the culture that have been the themes of the global questions used in the interview.

The summary may reveal gaps in the information needed to deliver a service, thereby pointing to areas for further ethnographic exploration in future contacts. Another value of the ethnographic summary is that the social worker obtains an initial assessment from the person and this data can be viewed as the person's explanatory model related to the presenting problem.

When ethnographic interviewing is done on a consistent basis, the social worker compiles a personal guidebook reflecting the person's culture. This guidebook can be added to as contacts continue with the person and others of the person's cultural group. Carefully prepared information on the person's cultural values, behaviors, and preferences—information that is continuously checked in repeated encounters—is basic to the effective delivery of service. Anything less means that social workers function in ignorance of what is really happening in the lives of their clients.

As we have noted, the best approach to the person's culture is through the person's own narrative. By letting the person teach the ways of his or her culture, a social worker can make a tactical advantage out of the cultural contrasts in the encounter. The social worker asks to be guided.

All ethnographic summaries will not be alike in content, which will depend on the social worker's choice of global questions and direction of the interview structure. The social worker ought to keep in mind throughout the interview that family relationships, help-seeking behaviors, child-rearing patterns, and physical and mental health issues are important areas around which to gather ethnographic information.

Finally, the ethnographic summary should incorporate information that may show a relationship between the preceding areas and the presenting problem from the person's perspective. By giving the social worker a picture of the person with the problem in the person's social context, the summary can become the instrument for negotiating a contract between the two. Once agreed on, this contract will define the nature of the problem and the intervention strategies to be utilized in the problem solution.

A carefully written ethnographic summary can be a vital contribution to the social agency's knowledge bank. Ethnographic summaries can be used by staff for in-service training sessions and in making culturally relevant interventions with clients of the contrasting group. Staff can also use the ethnographic summaries to discuss possible barriers within themselves to offering service to members of the cultural group.

Accumulated case data can be used to develop an agency profile of minority persons of color and their social views for fund-raising and policy-making efforts. Such data can be a convincing argument to advocate for a more sensitive approach to minority populations of color based on their perceptions of the impact of the social environment on self, family, and community. The accumulated data can aid in constructing a classification of client conditions, and possible treatment from a cultural perspective. A glossary of terms that would help social workers in cross-cultural encounters could be developed from accumulated ethnographic summaries related to a particular ethnic minority group.

The following is an illustration of an ethnographic summary.

Mrs. Hunter is not certain that her illness would be called Reye's Syndrome in Hong Kong. She states that in Hong Kong there are two levels of health care, one for the poor and one for the rich. The poor go to traditional doctors who treat people with Chinese herbs. The rich go to doctors who treat you like United States doctors. Doctors her friends would go to are like gods. If they tell you to do something, you do it without question. When women become ill, they are taken care of by the entire family. They would find a traditional doctor for the sick person and would pray for the sick person at a Buddhist temple. If necessary, someone would move in with the sick person to take care of them. This kind of help is considered a duty that everyone accepts. They do not complain. If a woman loses her husband, the first son will take on the responsibility of the family. Sons are very valuable because they also bring money into the family. Women work very hard; some work in a paid job as well as taking care of the home and children. Women are stingy but they make sure that there is money for the children's education. Children are taught to respect elders and have no rights at all. A woman should be able to tell her friends and neighbors about her troubles.

The stage is set for a dialogue based on the client's cultural perspectives. The focus of the dialogue will be agreement on a treatment plan that addresses some troublesome aspect of the client's life. The beginning narrative will serve the social worker as a framework for eliciting further information about the person's worldview within a relationship of acceptance. Through this entry point the social worker can begin a practice in which people make choices (King, 1995). The social worker's acceptance of the client's views, along with a clear understanding of his or her own cultural framework, leads to a capacity for cooperation as well as a capacity for understanding. In this sense the ethnographic model of interviewing goes beyond gaining understanding of the client. The process should lead to the establishment of cooperation in the problem solving endeavors (Levin, 1993).

The ethnographic interviewing process can be an important factor in the development of a trusting relationship necessary for the delivery of a culturally competent social service. Interviewing based on an ethnographic model of communication reveals data that is useful in treatment planning and interventions. Levinson, Merrifield, and Berg (1967, 402) speak to the negotiated consensus model of treatment planning in which complementary roles are present. Each person takes seriously the views of the other. Views of the client are elicited through the ethnographic interviewing model steps, which enable the social worker to enter into the world of the client rather than look at the world of the client. When addressing the possible interventions and treatment plan, the social worker begins a process of dialogue that will characterize the discussion. The foundation of this dialogue will be what the social worker has learned by having the client become a teacher.

REFERENCES

Ellison, Ralph. (1952). *Invisible man*. New York: Random House.

King, Joseph. (1995). *Narratives of possibility: Social movements, collective stories and the dilemmas of practice*. Paper presented at the New Social Movement and Community Organizing Conference, School of Social Work, University of Washington.

Levin, Jerome David. (1993). *Slings and arrows: Narcissistic injury and its treatment*. Northvale, NJ: Jason Aronson.

Levinson, Daniel, Merrifield, John, & Berg, Kenneth. (1967). Becoming a patient. *Archives of General Psychiatry, 17*, 385–406.

Melton, Lucy Ann. (1980). Introduction. In John Langston Gwaltney, *Drylongso: A portrait of black America* (pp. xxiv). New York: Random House.

APPENDICES

*The human being . . . cannot be touched in any
way that counts unless the word gets through to him
that he is being experienced as a human being by the
person for whom he is the subject of good works.*
—HOWARD THURMAN (1965). *The Luminous Darkness.*

Falling Out of the Model
Evaluating Self

One form of evaluation of social work practice is for the social worker to reflect on their communication process in the interview. Self-evaluation can result in the social worker learning about his or her individual effectiveness and performance. The following statement is illustrative of this evaluation method:

In my first interview with Mr. H., a 40-year-old, African American male at the shelter, he said he needed money so that he could rent a room and medical coverage so he could get medical care for his arthritis. He also said that he might have to think in terms of changing his lifestyle because of his medical condition. In the second interview I followed the interview process based on an ethnographic framework. I found this approach to communication useful for a number of reasons. It helped dissolve the hierarchy typical of the worker/client relationship. It helped me understand some of Mr. H.'s own priorities that he saw for himself as a member of a homeless culture of men. The approach also provided me with information that will be very useful in working as a partner with him in the problem-solving efforts.

Mr. H. taking the role of teacher and instructor and my taking the role of learner shortened the distance between us. I had some initial thoughts that this role shift would be troublesome as it meant that I would have to give up control of the interview. In the process I found that this was possible without me losing my essential role as a social worker. I was able to begin to view Mr. H. as an individual not a homeless person in need of social services. His life took on a texture and complexity rather than just a person with a problem to be solved or an applicant for service with a set of nondistinctive difficulties. There was a casualness in the interview I had not experienced in previous interviews with clients.

From the interview I began to understand why Mr. H. wanted a room of his own, the basis for viewing his medical problems as separate from his drinking problems, and his identification with other men who shared his way of life. I was able to experience how culture gives Mr. H. an identity and a set of rules which allows him to survive.

In our conversation Mr. H. revealed codes of behavior that I need to keep in mind as we progress further into our contacts. He values reciprocity and will not stay around where he feels he is not welcome.

I found the interview experience to be exhilarating. I came away from the interview with a respect for Mr. H. and a feeling of closeness to him which I now know will have impact on my efforts to be of assistance to him

The process of the interview reveals the practitioner's skill in communicating for a purpose. It is the place where concepts and principles of practice are processed through the persona of the social worker.

While learning from the person receiving social services is an appealing concept for most social workers, it is more easily understood than put into practice in the ethnographic interview. While a strict adherence to the process of the ethnographic interview is desired, it is possible for the social worker to move in and out of the model during the interview. In fact, most social workers do. Reflection on the completed ethnographic interview will help the social worker understand and grasp the concepts and principles of the model. The social worker has to make the necessary verbal statements or questions that move the person into a true role of cultural guide.

When the social worker does not do this, falling out of the model occurs. Social workers will fall out of the model in process when first beginning to learn and use the ethnographic interviewing model. Skill is learned through repetition and practice. Analysis of the practice will reveal and give social workers insight into how they are moving toward mastery of the ethnographic interviewing model. Without analysis of one's own interview it will probably not be possible to thoroughly evaluate and discuss the development of communication skills. Therefore it is recommended that the social worker, as a minimum process, record the ethnographic interview as soon after the interview is completed as possible. Videotaping is recommended if possible, as the social worker will not only hear the words spoken, but also gain insight into nonverbal communications. They always occur.

An outside reviewer such as a supervisor or peer would bring to the interview analysis a more objective stance than would the social worker who does the ethnographic interview. A check sheet of the ethnographic interview process points has proved very helpful to social workers in analyzing their ethnographic interviews. The social worker would have to have some comfort in criticizing self and not feel vulnerable and threatened by adverse comments. To ensure the presence of trust and security in the evaluation session, the outside reviewer ought to have some creditability in ethnographic interviewing.

A systematic study of why social workers fall out of the model has not been done. Experience in teaching the model and reading transcripts and viewing videotapes of ethnographic interviews suggest some conditions that seem to be present when social workers do fall out of the model.

Skill development in ethnographic interviewing can be evaluated by the social work practitioner as a beginning step in the evaluation of the effect of practice. Falling out of the model occurs in the following situations:

1. When the social worker interprets the word or words of the cultural guide.
2. When the social worker begins to personalize the content prior to receiving full information on the cultural world of the cultural guide from the cultural guide.
3. When the content from the cultural guide seems to stir up an emotional response from the social worker and leads the social worker to normalize or be openly sympathetic and empathic.
4. When the content is socially threatening to the social worker.
5. When the social worker does not attend to the dynamics of the relationship.
6. When the social worker reveals difficulties in taking the role of learner and shifts to the role of a teacher or therapist or counselor or advocate.
7. When the cultural guide concept is not explained and an open agreement not reached in the ethnographic interview.
8. When the social worker gives an opinion or an evaluation of the cultural guide's content.
9. When the social worker asks only global questions and does not elicit descriptors of cover terms heard.
10. When the social worker begins to take a social history.
11. When the social worker blocks and struggles to get the ethnographic interview going again.
12. When the social worker tries to get descriptors for all cover terms and stops the interview so all words and descriptive material can be written down.
13. When the social worker asks the cultural guide to answer "What do you mean by. . . ?"

14. When the social worker continually focuses on the personal by using "you" rather than using words which will lead the cultural guide into explaining communal or group thoughts and behaviors.

The impact of the social environment on human identity and functioning in a multicultural society must be recognized by social workers in all fields of practice. Operationalizing the person-in-situation concept is greatly assisted by learning about the culture of the other. Social workers must be aware of their own cultural backgrounds because their backgrounds will influence all aspects of cross-cultural helping encounters. Lack of cultural self-awareness will result in failure to recognize or discover the importance and impact of culture in the lives of those they are called upon to help.

APPENDIX B

Self-Evaluation Form

Name _____

Ethnographic Interviewing Skills

At certain times, it is important that social workers review the ethnographic interviewing process and evaluate their own skill development.

1. Read through the list of skills and decide which ones you are doing all right, which ones you are not demonstrating, and which ones you need to improve on. Mark each item in the appropriate place.
2. Some skills that are important to you in becoming a skilled ethnographic interviewer may not be listed. You can identify and include them in your response to #3.
3. Go back over the list and write an evaluative summary of yourself as an ethnographic interviewer.

Skill	Doing all right	Not doing	Need work on
1. Understanding theory	_____	_____	_____
2 Writing global questions prior to the contact	_____	_____	_____
3. Engaging in friendly conversation	_____	_____	_____
4. Explaining process	_____	_____	_____
5. Explaining roles	_____	_____	_____
6. Explaining recording	_____	_____	_____
7. Native language explanations	_____	_____	_____
8. Question explanations	_____	_____	_____

  9. Asking the first global question _____ _____ _____
 10. Hearing cover words or phrases _____ _____ _____

Descriptive Questions (Werner & Schoepfle)
 11. Asking space questions _____ _____ _____
 12. Asking time questions _____ _____ _____
 13. Asking actor questions _____ _____ _____
 14. Asking evaluation questions _____ _____ _____

Descriptive Questions (Spradley)
 15. Asking typical questions _____ _____ _____
 16. Asking specific questions _____ _____ _____
 17. Asking guided questions _____ _____ _____
 18. Asking task-related questions _____ _____ _____
 19. Asking example questions _____ _____ _____
 20. Asking experience questions _____ _____ _____
 21. Asking native language questions _____ _____ _____
 22. Termination skills _____ _____ _____
 23. Writing the ethnographic summary _____ _____ _____
 24. My self-evaluation: _____ _____ _____

APPENDIX C

Assessment, Negotiated Consensus Treatment Planning, and Culturally Relevant Interventions and Treatment

The first stage of the helping process is information gathering. I have presented an alternative approach modeled on ethnographic interviewing. The recognition of other worldviews that reflect cultural patterns of group life follows consideration of alternative paradigms for knowing. I hope that the material previously presented will create another route to the effective delivery of social services to those who represent contrasting ways of viewing the world. A basic assumption has been that how we view the world and the people in it effects the process and practice of social work. I have offered an alternative paradigm to traditional social work paradigms, fully aware of "the ambiguous waters of new paradigms for creating, communicating and expanding knowledge-creation processes" (Shriver, 1995, xi). In this appendix, three areas—assessment, negotiated consensus treatment planning, and culturally relevant interventions and treatment—are considered.

ASSESSMENT

The process of assessment has often been a controversial issue in cross-cultural social work practice. Assessment is generally viewed as giving meaning to information gained through the interview process. At times, assessment waits until sufficient information is gathered to make a decision about what the information means from a psycho-social perspective. At other times, assessments are made immediately after the interview. The important variable is what decisions must be made relative to the presenting problem.

The assessment, according to most social work scholars, is not to be seen as a permanent indication of thinking cast in concrete, but as a flexible summary that can be changed as more information is gained by the social worker in the course of the helping process.

In traditional practice frameworks, the assessment decisions emanate from the social worker's body of knowledge and are independent of the person seeking help. The social worker's frame of reference is paramount. Difficulties will occur as the social worker's perceptual screen does not match the perceptual screen of the potential client. Due to the distinct cultural contrasts between a dominant culture social worker and an ethnic minority person, the assessment and resulting treatment plan can be particularly troublesome in cross-cultural social work practices. Leigh (1985, 455) asserts that

> Assessments of minority clients are often limited because of a lack of cultural understanding, and social services to such clients are predicated on incomplete knowledge of the minority client's circumstances, strengths, resources, motivations, and problems. Interventions based on such incomplete assessments will not be operative.

In order to avoid this problem, the social worker must consider the views of the person in the assessment process. Even when hearing the person's self-evaluative opinions, many times the social worker questions the judgment of the person and discounts what the person states (Kagle, 1988, 37).

The assessment process is pivotal. Unless an accurate assessment is obtained and formulated, treatment is irrelevant and, at worst, harmful. Assessment, according to Meyer (1985), is a process of understanding a problem. The unit of attention can be the individual, the family, or the community. The accuracy of the assessment is highly dependent on the agency's function—its stage of development as a community agency—and the skill and focus of the social worker. The assessment should reflect a shared understanding, not just a professional judgment (Seabury, 1985, 348).

Following the naturalistic inquiry framework, assessment would view the information gathered as related to the problem. The purpose of an assessment would be to determine what factors are involved in the situation and what must be done to solve the problem. Rodewell (1987, 241) advances the idea that naturalistic inquiry is a means to offset the problems that social workers have encountered using other assessment frameworks. The assessment in this model is the result of an effort on the part of the social worker whereby time is allowed for the social worker to engage the person in a culturally focused conversation. A provisional report is developed early in the contacts and is shared with the client to obtain confirmation of the accuracy of the social worker's perception of the perspectives the person represents. The assessment process then becomes a process of negotiation with all parties agreeing. The goal of this frame for assessment is to promote understanding, which is a product of the interaction, not a record of the social worker's professionally accepted understanding of data. This framework takes into account the explanatory models of the person, the social worker, and the agency. An understanding of explanatory models will clarify this line of thinking.

Explanatory Models

People develop systems of thought to explain the world and continually test out these thoughts for revision if they do not find them accurate in giving meaning to their experiences. These systems are guides from which people make sense out of experiences that are changing and dynamic. They differ between individuals as each person interprets experience according to a complicated system of judgments even within that person's culture. Explanatory models develop from which the person constructs worldviews of a global and a specific nature. They are transient, not fixed, changing as the nature of the experience changes and as they provide, or fail to provide, an adequate explanation of the experience. They are paradigms that can be articulated. They are based on some theory of causation and behavior. In helping situations, the person's, the social worker's, and the agency's explanatory models are always present. An explanatory model of each can be formulated using the following steps:

1. What is the presenting problem?
2. What is the cause of the problem?
3. What is the solution to the problem?
4. What resources are needed to solve the problem?
5. What are the barriers to problem solving?

The Person's Explanatory Model

The person's explanatory model is contained in the ethnographic data that comprises the ethnographic summary. By taking the ethnographic data and relating it to the outline, the social worker can gain knowledge of the person's cultural construct system. The content of the person's explanatory model will have direct reference to the areas on which the social worker focuses the ethnographic interview. It can reveal the person's definition of the problem, the cultural meaning of the problem, and the person's perceptual set regarding the problem. The summary can also contain information about the person's family relationships, help-seeking behaviors, child-rearing practices, and approaches to health issues. The cultural meanings and values attached to each of these areas may also be revealed and will have relevance to the presenting problem.

Kleinman (1978, 256) suggests that, in health care settings, the person's explanatory model can be elicited by asking direct questions such as (1) "What do you think caused your problem?" (2) "Why do you think it started when it did?" (3) "What do you think your sickness does to you?" (4) "How severe is your illness?" (5) "Will it have a long or short course?" (6) "What kind of treatment do you think you should receive?" (7) "What is the most important result you think you will receive from treatment?" (8) "What do you fear most about the treatment?" These questions can form a reference point for exploring other explanatory models presented to social workers and can be cast in the form of ethnographic questions for use during the ethnographic interview.

The person's explanatory model as contained in the ethnographic summary is illustrated in the following:

> Helen is a thirty-five-year-old Native American, referred by her doctor, who needs assistance with housing and medical payments. She states she is not as concerned for herself as she is for other Native American women who are worse off than herself. She says their problems stem from being Native American in a white society. She views herself as being a host to all who come to the United States. She says she respects diversity because Native people are so diverse. She believes that a Native person in a white culture must be of two worlds and must be able to move easily between the two. She believes that everything in the country is hers yet must be shared with others.
>
> Native people move back and forth between two worlds. Their survival depends on how well they learn to do this. Society has inflicted spiritual and political damage on Native people and this creates health and social problems in her tribe. Helen believes that the answer to these problems is for Native people to work within the political system.
>
> She represents her people in everything she does. The Native family is "we" focused, "me" is "we." The tribe's history is their cultural identity. Time, as a straight line, is not part of Native culture. The Native perspective of time is as a circle; family of the past and present are the same.

In this ethnographic summary, Helen's explanatory model reveals crucial issues about herself and her cultural group. Helen has a view of the causes of, and solutions to her cultural group's problems. All of this information is important and can only be obtained through attempts to elicit Helen's own explanatory model.

The Social Worker's Explanatory Model

Even prior to contact with the person, the social worker has developed an explanatory model of the problem to be presented or of the person who will present the problem. This occurs as a result of socialization to the profession, formal education, personal history, or informal education. In this sense, the social worker is no different from all other members of society who also have constructs to bring meaning into their worlds. In addition, the social worker may have secondary information from the referral that will influence the thinking process. Ashby (1990) urges social workers to write down their explanatory model of each case problem before seeing the person, as this will aid in surfacing the social workers' predisposition to the case.

This initial explanatory model is strictly the social worker's perceptions based on whatever information the social worker has in mind at the point of referral. From this natural cognitive process of evaluating a case situation, the social worker begins to pull from within self an inclination to move in a certain direction in the helping process. It is an arbitrary process but it forces the social worker to develop questions of a global nature to bring to the ethnographic interview. The social worker essentially becomes a researcher, testing out his or her own hypothesis, which may contain bias and prejudices that will be present in the social worker's contact with the person.

After obtaining the person's explanatory model and being aware of his or her own, the social worker should study the two models for similarities and differences. Do the person and the social worker agree on how the problem can be solved? These issues and others should be easily ascertainable. The closer the two explanatory models, the easier it may be to arrive at an agreeable treatment plan.

Because the ethnographic interview process is a teaching and learning process with the social worker in the role of student, the social worker must redo or revise his or her explanatory model based on the ethnographic data. In rethinking, the social worker may well discover that his or her original explanatory model is no longer valid. At a minimum, the social worker ought to discover that the second explanatory model moves closer to the person's. If it does not, problems will occur in carrying out a treatment plan. If the social worker does not have congruency with the person, he or she might have to refer the person to another social worker who is more attuned to listening to and incorporating the constructs of that person. Lack of congruence may be due to the social distance, differing life circumstances, and differing status of the person and the social worker. Marked differences that surface through this process need to be evaluated carefully. If the social worker thinks movement toward the person's constructs can be incorporated, then the opportunity is available to move toward the negotiated model of treatment planning.

For social workers, awareness of their explanatory models, which may reflect commonly held professional explanatory models, may lead them to clarify areas of their own professional explanatory models. Social workers can identify areas of similarities and differences, which can become part of the process of helping in interviews.

The Agency's Explanatory Model

The social agency is among the factors that impact services to clients. Kagle (1988, 35) states that "social workers are also affected by the organizations in which they work and by their role as professionals in society. An important function of the helping profession and of social services is to promote compliance with prevailing institutional and societal norms." These social norms become part of the agency's mandate and influence strongly the explanatory model of the social services offered by the agency.

The agency's explanatory model is generally embedded in the agency's mission statement and policies, which govern the approaches to help, as well as the resources the agency makes available to social workers. The acceptable approaches to treatment and understanding of people and problems can also be discovered by social workers as they become familiar with the agency's administrative policies that govern caseloads, time issues, and accountability issues.

It should be noted that the agency's explanatory model can be elusive to the social worker. The social worker is urged to learn about the agency's policies, history, and rates of success with ethnic minority persons. Intake procedures, preferred clients, and social worker employment attributes and qualifications all have implications for learning about the agency's explanatory model. How does the agency view the persons it serves?

While the social worker may focus on issues related to the person's perceptions and views of the presenting problem, often the ethnographic data will be of such a nature that it will be more global in relation to the person's perceptions of self in society. Much of the ethnographic data will be in the realm of educating the social worker to the cultural imperatives of the person's construct system. This kind of data will assist the social worker in looking at life through the lens of the person in that life. The data important to explanatory models will be a part of that broader perspective.

NEGOTIATED CONSENSUS

Treatment planning involves a mutual discussion around the explanatory models of the social worker, the person, and the agency. In consideration of the agency's explanatory model, the social worker must consider the presenting problem of the person and what possible approaches and solutions are acceptable to the agency within its established practices, procedures, programs, and policies. The social worker may construct a list of alternative approaches that are appropriate to the agency's service structure. Important to this process of thinking are the resources available *within* the agency to solve the presenting problem. Referral as a treatment alternative may be considered if it is thought that the agency practices, approaches, and programs are inadequate to meet the service needs of the case. This decision does not, and must not, however, rest on the agency explanatory model only. The treatment plan must take into consideration the explanatory models of the person and the social worker as well. The social worker's explanatory model is the first constructed, prior to the beginning contacts. The person's explanatory model is discovered through the ethnographic focus of the interview. Once the ethnographic summary is completed, social workers should return to a consideration of their own explanatory model and the agency's explanatory model as they relate to the person's explanatory model. The social worker may discover areas of disagreement or agreement about possible solutions and treatment approaches among the three explanatory models.

The social worker should always search for commonalties between the three explanatory models in order to initiate an effective intervention. The social worker, rather than making a decision unilaterally, should consider entering into a negotiated process of treatment planning with the person. This is often a necessary step in the treatment planning process. A unilateral decision too often reflects the cultural bias of the social worker and the agency and can lead to inappropriate treatment for the problem presented.

In the next in-person contact, the social worker should present the explanatory models to the person and enter into a discussion of the possible approaches that all three explanatory models suggest. At times, the ethnographic summary may not contain material directly related to the person's explanatory model of the presenting problem. The worldviews of the person will sensitize the social worker to the person's culture and help the social worker understand the person as a cultural being. Social workers should be aware of cultural information related to the presenting problem and of cultural information related more generally to the cultural world of the person.

During the interview, the social worker has the opportunity to feed back to the person, acting as a cultural guide, the cultural imperatives the social worker has learned about the person. The person who has been the focus of learning through the elicited ethnographic data, then can be self-corrective as to what the social worker learned and can have the opportunity to consider alternative solutions to the presenting problem based on the multiple meanings of the data and the right of refusal. The social worker reports to the person the results of this complicated thinking process. The social worker presents honestly his or her thoughts about the nature of the problem as it is modified by the person's explanatory model and the agency's explanatory model. The person is given the opportunity to reflect on the professional's statements and choose, if necessary, from alternative solutions. The goal of the interview is to reach an agreement about treatment. This agreement becomes the initial treatment plan and, once completed, the person formally enters into the role of client. This stage may take more than one interview as the person's decision should be based on a complete understanding of alternate solutions, the meanings of such solutions, and the costs of each alternative solution. Social workers must be cautious that they do not allow their own theories to block mutual decision making or try to make the client's problems conform to their theories. Through careful listening, the social worker paves the way for the necessary negotiation process. The social worker in the contact strives for nontacit, open approval of the person. Tacit approval may be given by the person because the person may feel "this" is a solution in order to achieve another end. If the person has no choices, the social worker should clearly state this fact. The solution may lie in the area of personal change or in changing aspects of the social environment or both. How this is decided has strong implications for the treatment strategies agreed on by the social worker and the person.

The Issue of Congruency

Whatever the agreed upon solution, the treatment plan must be viewed as congruent to the person if it is to have a chance at successfully resolving the problem. The person may have difficulty with a proposed treatment plan when the plan involves values that are at odds with his or her cultural values or represents deviations from the group norms aspired to by the individual. The person may be more amiable to the treatment plan of the social worker and agency when the person is not a true "behavioral ethnic" and is already seeking to be acculturated into the societal group represented by the dominant culture social worker (Anderson, 1989). The person may be in agreement with the social worker's and agency's explanatory models when the person is experiencing a psychological crisis, feeling that all known cultural problem-solving efforts have failed to provide the solution.

It may be impossible for the person to consider the social worker's or the agency's explanatory model. (Presenting these two explanatory models as one model, not differentiating one from the other in the discussion, should be avoided.) The resultant treatment plan, when the person has no faith in the solutions that are presented, is not appropriate. The person may have known others in the same minority culture group for whom these solutions have already been tried and found wanting. The person may even have tried the suggested solutions and approaches and found them to be lacking in the power to solve the problem.

The factor of congruency must be kept in mind by the social worker. Rather than viewing treatment planning as a process of decision making on the part of the social worker and agreement on the part of the person, the treatment planning should be viewed as a process of help in and of itself. Participation in treatment planning through a negotiated consensus model is empowering as the person becomes an active participant in the process.

Culturally sensitive treatment planning and intervention procedures must be cognizant of sources of strain or gaps between a minority culture value or precept and an underlying dominant culture value. Culturally sensitive strategies must be employed to carry out interventions. For example, consider the problem of removing a child from a home whose culture places a high value on children and sees child rearing as a major adult responsibility. In this situation, the parents are shamed in their community. A true behavioral ethnic can be expected to utilize whatever honorable solutions or actions are used by his or her group when they are found wanting in this important area. A prime factor to be remembered by the social worker is to try to discover culturally appropriate methods of helping and then to use them if possible.

The Negotiation Process

Kenmore (1987) addresses the prospect of negotiated consensus regarding planning and intervention. Kenmore (1987, 140–141) states:

> Empirical investigation of worker experience strongly suggests that the negotiation process is a real and important aspect of initial contact with clients. Analysis of worker experience further suggests that the relationship between practice principles and practice experience of negotiation is complex and indirect. At least three areas of intervening influence emerge as important in this relationship. First, worker adherence to agency practice philosophy is certainly an influential factor in the initial selection and use of practice principles. Second, persistence and strength of client opposition to the worker's preferred practice approach eventually exert strong influences on the worker's willingness to alter practice preferences.
>
> Finally, worker discomfort with uncertainty related to conflict with clients over competing practice preferences is a strong motivation to achieve an intervention contract. The need of the worker to experience success and progress in each case appears to cause a shift in loyalty away from adherence to the approach preferred by the agency and toward an approach preferred by clients.

The need for the social worker to achieve success and progress can be a strong motivating force for the social worker to move toward client preference in treatment approaches. While this dynamic may operate, there may also be other contingent factors, such as the nearness of the explanatory models or the insistence of the client on his or her method of problem solving. The social worker may go along with the client treatment preference out of discomfort or frustration, growing out of not understanding the person or out of a feeling of being stuck and having no other alternatives. On the other hand, the social worker may be unwilling to relinquish the power of decision making and may not adhere to client treatment preference. Social workers need to be clear about the reasons why they are adhering or not adhering to the treatment preferences of their clients.

In the ethnographic framework, the social worker is advised to adhere initially to the solution suggested by the person rather than by the agency's or the social worker's preferred ways of treatment. The self-determination principle is operative.

"The historically central professional value of client self-determination suggests that the difference between social workers and clients about expectations of treatment should be resolved in the direction of client preference" (Kenmore, 1987, 142). It must be noted that negotiated agreements imply an equality of power and responsibility. The ethnographic interview process sets up a different role relationship between the social worker and the person in which the role reversal implies a sharing of power. The negotiated contracting process is an extension of this relationship of mutuality through open sharing and conjoint decision making (Rojek and Collins, 1987).

Seabury (1979) supports negotiated contracting as a mutual decision-making process, which can be verbal or written. If necessary, differences in explanatory models should be discussed and conflict managed if these differences will create barriers to an agreement. Seabury (38) writes:

> Some workers are unable to contract successfully with clients because of their own perceptions of "competent" practice. They may perceive themselves as having a special, professional expertise; they do not see any merit in "bargaining" with a client (after all, the client may be the one who caused the problem in the first place); and they are unable to establish any parity in the decision-making process. These workers believe that the right contract is the one their professional judgment dictates and that, until the client "sees the light" and stops resisting the worker's suggestions, service will not proceed productively.

The social worker who strives for success in helping others will use professional communication to facilitate client participation. The social worker shares professional judgment but the content of the decision is not as important as the person's participation in the decision-making process. Maluccio and Marlow (1974) are of the opinion that dealing with discrepancies in explanatory models results in a feeling of greater mutuality and role complementarity, which can only enhance the helping interactions.

Levinson, Merrifield, and Berg (1967) were early exponents of the negotiated model of treatment planning. In their model, the social worker enters into a relationship with the person regarding the nature of the services and the source of the problem, the kinds of services that may be helpful, what the agency can offer, and what alternates are available for help. The social worker and the person take seriously the views of each other. They try to arrive at a mutual decision as to what will happen in the way of treatment. This encounter is viewed as a bilateral negotiation rather than as an event governed by unilateral control by the social worker. The person is seen as an applicant for service and not until an agreement is reached regarding treatment is the person designated a client (Alcabes and Jones, 1985). The negotiated model of consensus for treatment planning is characterized by clarifying the problem areas, searching for the relevant means of help, exchanging information, acknowledging the limitations of each party, and developing genuine mutual understanding.

CULTURALLY RELEVENT INTERVENTIONS AND TREATMENT

If we are to be serious about engaging in culturally relevant interventions and treatment of people who are ethnically different from ourselves, we must be serious about learning about the belief systems of people in any given cultural group. We need to know what the belief systems are, how they operate, for what reasons they operate, and what their place is in the life of the group and in the life of each individual who is a member of that group. We need to know this because it is within these belief systems that we can find the explanations of the responses to life stresses and the prescriptions for what to do about them. For example, a white male social worker using an ethnographic interviewing approach recorded the following details in an interview with an African American male regarding how his reference group belief system views physical symptoms.

> I grew up in the church of Metaphysics and a family steeped in occultism and a lot of rituals to handle problems. My grandmother was both a minister of the gospel and an occult practitioner.
> In my family there is a tale told to everyone. My great, great grandmother has a snake placed inside her body. This snake was

visible on the side of her throat. Apparently it was supposed to have been done by a woman because of some jealous feud or something between my great, great grandmother and her.

Some family member found a practitioner to remove the snake from great, great grandmother. When it had finally been arranged to have the ceremony, the practitioner, occultist, or madam, as they were sometimes called, had an accident and suddenly died. It is not clear what happened but my family thinks it was a curse put on her for trying to remove the snake.

My great, great grandmother was stuck with this snake in her throat. Until she died, she carried that snake, which you could visibly see, according to all the women in my family, and which caused my grandmother to constantly go around clearing her throat.

As a result of this, we believe that this is why my brother, my sister, and myself have this habit of clearing our throats. When we get colds, we believe the snake is in our throats and we are the target of someone's jealous curse. To get rid of the cold, we have to go around and find the person who we have made jealous and say that we are sorry. When you do that, the cold goes away.

In my community, you hear a lot about such situations. They are told to you and spoken about in normal conversation. Clairvoyance was and is commonplace. People are always saying "You know they say Mrs. Jones can see things." I believe she can. I believe in clairvoyance because I come from a long line of people like that. We all have a capacity for it.

A lady friend of mine visits with her dead husband. She has a boyfriend and one night when she was asleep in her bed, she suddenly woke up. She sat up in bed and looked at the foot of the bed and saw her dead husband sitting there. Her dead husband began to talk to her about some business matters and how she could contact his sister and obtain certain documents she needed. He also warned her about certain matters concerning their children. He told her how to treat the younger son's asthma. He then disappeared.

Later the same day, she told her boyfriend about her late husband's visit. He laughed. Soon after, her youngest son told her that he was visited by his late father. His father kissed him and told him his mother was going to do something to relieve his asthma. The lady was relieved to hear this but did not tell of her experience with her late husband. She contacted her sister-in-law and the documents were exactly as her late husband had told her. Her sister-in-law was shocked to learn that the lady knew where the documents were as only she and her brother knew about them.

As we consider the area of culturally relevant interventions and treatment, we have to agree that we want to be a part of a community of persons who create good. No matter what the movement in our helping efforts toward achieving success, we are driven to becoming better at what we do. We are "unfinished," always in process, because of the changing demands to meet the social service needs of a changing world and changing people situations. An important issue arises: having to use ourselves as helpers in such a manner that our help makes sense to the people who request our assistance. We know that people are not cut from the same cloth. Each of us is unique, and the challenge to understand other people is even greater when consideration is given to people who represent a cultural contrast to ourselves. Critics have argued convincingly that social services offered to ethnic minority persons have suffered as a result of social workers from the dominant culture being insensitive to ethnic minority cultures. Professional interventions and treatment are thought to be offered out of the social worker's personal or professional cultural frame of reference. Even more criticism has been directed toward practice procedures that are felt to be imposed on ethnic minorities and to be alien to their accepted methods of problem solving (Kleinman, 1988; Green, 1982; Atkinson, Morten and Sue, 1989).

In response to years of criticism, efforts have been made to address the issue of culturally relevant interventions and treatments that take into consideration knowledge about the worldview of the ethnic minority person. Crystal (1989, 410) asserts that a keen awareness of the cultural framework of the ethnic minority group is necessary if interventions and treatment will serve positively in the problem-solving effort. For example, culturally relevant interventions with Asian Americans ought to be based on knowledge of how Asian Americans define problems within their own cultural group. Activities of the social worker based on such knowledge are known as *culturally relevant* interventions and treatment.

Thus, culturally relevant interventions and treatment have a base in cultural knowledge related to communication patterns, family dynamics, roles that people play, support networks, and help-seeking behaviors. Other areas that can be learned by ethnographic interviewing techniques are the rules that govern behavior, religious rites, and roles that people assume in times of trouble. Lewis (1985) suggests that such gained knowledge has the effect of assisting the social worker in looking through the eyes of the culture bearer. Only when this occurs can empathy be established in the working relationship. If this does not occur, all interventions and treatment are not culturally congruent. They can also be termed *insensitive* and *irrelevant*.

The crucial phase of the helping process is what the social worker does to help (treatment) and how the social worker uses self (interventions) in the process of help. Social workers must "do" in addition to understanding. Understanding, while necessary, is not enough truly to enable the ethnic minority person in problem-solving efforts. The social worker may learn much about the cultural life of a group and become very conversant on the cultural group. That does not mean, however, that the social worker "acts" or "does" consistently within the group's cultural framework. In fact, the social worker may use knowledge of the group in a manner that has a negative impact on the person and the group. For these reasons, culturally relevant interventions and treatment become a crucial practice issue when working across the cultural gap.

Interventions

In the initial stages of the helping process in cross-cultural practice situations, the formation of the helping relationship is a major focus. How this relationship is developed can be viewed within a cultural framework. Western Apache culture, according to Basso (1970), informs us that Western Apaches encounter strangers by restraint in talking, as they consider the establishment of a relationship to be a serious matter. Due to this cultural factor, the social worker moving into a relationship of help should speak first. LaFromboise and Dixon (1981) further suggest that the social worker not refer to time restraints on the contact until the final moments of the first meeting. To do so would be a demonstration of insensitivity to the Native American culture and would be a nontrustworthy intervention. Similarly, African Americans are sensitive to strangers' use of first names in first encounters. If they are called by a first name without permission, African Americans interpret this action as negative and demeaning.

Interventions are intrusions into an observed process between the social worker and the person. Interventions can be activities that are demonstrated in the interview to bring about a desired change. Ashby and Leigh (1990) view interventions as uninvited actions or acts of nonagreed upon behaviors. Interventions are those activities that the social worker demonstrates in the interview.

Interventions are generally verbal in nature and occur in the communications process. Interventions that are culturally congruent may be noted in the following illustration:

> When the mental health worker first introduced me to Mrs. Chan, Mrs. Chan's reaction was mixed with shame and hopefulness. She remarked that she was "losing face" because of her situation (depression, loss of weight, and energy) and regretted greatly that she has to be a "burden" to me. I replied that I considered it a privilege and rare opportunity to be of assistance to her. I added that my deceased mother's maiden name was the same as her last name. Mrs. Chan relaxed and remarked that my mother must be very proud of me. I thanked her. I then thanked the mental health worker for introduc-

ing me to Mrs. Chan. As soon as the mental health worker left, Mrs. Chan began to prepare tea for me. I immediately volunteered to help her. (Ho, 1982, 6)

In this illustration, the social worker intervened into the communication process on the basis of his understanding and knowledge of Chinese cultural frameworks for the meaning of having problems, family relationships, attitudes, attributes of helpers, and the roles of older and younger persons within the culture. In other situations where the social worker has no knowledge of the cultural imperatives of the person, ethnographic interviewing procedures are of assistance in learning the person's cultural framework. In such situations, the social worker might also follow the lead of the person in terms of appropriate acts. For example, the acceptance of an offer of food when making a home visit may demonstrate an openness to the cultural norms of the person. Interventions that are culturally congruent, verbal, and uninvited demonstrate a high level of cross-cultural competence.

Culturally relevant interventions are those acts made by the social worker that vary from minute social gestures, which can create barriers to relationship formation, to very complex interactions initiated to solve problems, change behaviors, alleviate distress, and change thinking. These actions must be within the cultural framework of the ethnic minority person and must be experienced as culturally congruent. The social worker has to examine his or her own culturally sanctioned practices and become alert to whether these practices are irrelevant or inadequate for the ethnic minority person (Levine and Padilla, 1980, ll).

LaFromboise and Dixon (1981, 136) state that nontrustworthy interventions by the social worker working with Native Americans can be illustrated by the following:

1. Abrupt shifts of topics.
2. Inaccurate paraphrases.
3. Mood changes and interest changes.
4. Break in confidentiality.
5. Stereotyped statements.
6. Broken promises.

Each of these actions by the social worker in the interview is not culturally congruent to the person and will affect their ability to form a beneficial relationship.

Treatment

Treatment as defined by Perlman (1957, 181) is "doing with or subjecting to some action." The social worker must view cultural material as especially viable knowledge and use it as a base for treatment. An essential aspect of treatment of the culturally contrasting client is that it must be arrived at through a mutual process of discovery (Ashby, 1990).

The social worker in cross-cultural practice will strive to discover what are the person's culturally accepted ways of problem solving. The social worker then will use these culturally relevant problem-solving methods to solve the person's particular problem. These culturally acceptable treatments may be dream interpretations, herbal remedies, purification rites, and other practices not considered mainstream problem-solving techniques. Such use of culturally appropriate problem-solving solutions should be part of the ethnic minorities' informal or formal cultural structures. These solutions may occur spontaneously with their own indigenous helpers with whom the social worker may have to work within a collaborative arrangement.

Lantz and Pegram (1989) studied the procedures that indigenous helpers use in their curative practices. These may be important for the social worker to understand in order to consider adopting some aspects of curative factors in his or her work with ethnically different, minority persons. These curative factors are treatment procedures or activities that have been shown to be helpful in many different cultures (Lewis, 1974; Levine and Padilla, 1980, 11). Eight curative factors were isolated in Lantz and Pegram's study:

1. *Physical Intervention.* Medications and surgery are curative factors in most Western cultures. In other cultures, medicine and surgery are curative factors but they are provided for symbolic, sacred, and cathartic reasons, not for bio-chemical imbalance reasons. (56)

2. *World View Respect.* No healing even of a psychological nature works unless the methods of helping are compatible with the person's world view. World view compatibility must exist between the social worker and the person if effective helping is to occur. For example, medication may not fit a person's world view unless the persons giving the medication are blessed. Out of respect for a person's world view, social workers might consider having their work blessed by an important person in the person's life. (56–57)

3. *Hope.* While hope can be an illusive concept to social workers, it is an important curative factor. The more the person has hope in the power of the helping person or in the potential for help, the greater the positive prognosis. Symbols such as diplomas, awards, testimonials of persons who have been helped all have the power to give hope in the healing process. (57)

4. *Helper Attractiveness.* The person's perception of the social worker's ability to help is important. The length of training and where one trained along with a presentation of self that is accepting, warm, and mature, adds to the helper's attractiveness. Helper attractiveness is dependent upon world view respect and the attributes of the helper congruent to the culture of the person. (58–59)

5. *Control.* This curative factor relates to the person learning something in the process of help which can be used to master problems as they will occur in the future. Persons can be taught techniques to master anxiety that are culturally appropriate such as how to ward off evil or how to use insights gained into self to manage relationship problems. (59–60)

6. *Rites of Initiation.* The person is asked to give up on old patterns of behavior in exchange for new ones during rituals such as ceremonies marking life transitions or the movement from one development stage to another. (60–61)

7. *Cleansing Experiences.* In this curative area, the person is cleansed of past mistakes and failures through purification rites such as the use of the "sweat house," which can help in overcoming guilt, sadness, and depression. A cleansing experience can also be used for initiation into a new form of living. Testimonies in public about past ill-conceived ways of dealing with problems along with the successful ways of managing problems, can also be cleansing experiences. (61–63)

8. *Existential Realization.* This occurs when the social worker helps the person discover the meanings of and in an experience. The helper facilitates a reflective stance from which the person examines self in relation to others in the culture, or in relation to his or her own inner thinking and overt behavior. In other situations of existential curing, the helper facilitates the person's regaining of soul through dealing with the secular demands which are used as a cover for the true self. (63–67)

Once the social worker understands these curative factors, he or she may apply them to any ethnic cultural group. The social worker needs to determine if the curative procedures accepted by a particular ethnic culture group can be used within the formal helping system of the social worker or must be done by a healer or helper within the ethnic cultural group. The case of an African American woman is cited by Lanz and Pegram (56–57) to illustrate how curative thinking can be applied in a formal helping situation. The African American woman wanted to leave her husband due to his physical abuse of her but felt she could not because her husband had hired a root woman to hex her. Treatment planning accepted this worldview, and, along with supportive services, linked the woman with a folk healer who took the hex off her, permitting her to leave the abusive situation. Worldview respect may also improve the social worker's attractiveness and aid in the installation of hope.

Curative procedures are important in the treatment of problems of ethnic minority persons. The social worker may have to consider rites and rituals. When utilizing culturally congruent treatment procedures, the social worker may not only have to work with indigenous helpers, but also may have to discover who they are and where they are in the community. The social worker may have to convince them to be part of a treatment team to which they may not be sympathetic. The social worker ascertains whether the ethnic minority person views the use of an indigenous helper as viable. After discussion and evaluation with the ethnic minority person, the social worker may blend mainstream treatment forms with helping that is closer to ethnic cultural group norms (Whittaker and Tracy, 1989).

Not all treatment of culturally contrasting persons will be done through indigenous helpers. It is the task of the social worker to gather appropriate cultural information by ethnographic means and then, in concert with the person, to decide on the appropriate treatment procedures. If there is a question about the cultural appropriateness of the treatment, the social worker should first try a treatment that is more congruent with the culture of the client.

In the process of arriving at culturally congruent treatment procedures, the social worker is advised to remember that even the most minute interventions are important. If some interventions are not culturally acceptable, the social worker will not have the full cooperation of the ethnic minority person in treatment. Many times in health care settings, ethnic persons of different cultures are found to be noncompliant because of culturally insensitive interventions they experienced in the process of getting help.

This may even occur when the ethnic minority person seemingly is part of the larger cultural system. Very often ethnic minority persons live in two cultures but their major cultural reference is their own ethnic cultural group. Opportunities to interact with the larger culture may only occur at work or in public places, such as stores and buildings. Due to their cultural and racial contrasts from the larger society, even these places may not be supportive of the minority position in society. The comfort zone is identified within the ethnic minority culture. Therefore, the culture of the ethnic minority person is viable and operative in spite of a parallel existence in the larger society and with other ethnic groups. The important dynamic for the social worker to consider in cross-cultural contacts is whether his or her cultural framework will affect the client's primary cultural form. Interaction with a culture is not the same as living in a culture. A crucial juncture in cross-cultural practice is the intervention and treatment phase of the helping process. Which person's worldview will predominate in this process is key to effective helping for the person who represents cultural contrasts.

REFERENCES

Alcabes, Abraham, & Jones, James A. (1985). Structural determinants of "clienthood." *Social Work*, 30(1),49–56.

Anderson, James R. (1989). Personal correspondence.

Ashby, Marianne. (1990). *What is cultural treatment?* Unpublished manuscript.

Ashby, Marianne, & Leigh, James W. (1990). *The three phases of the explanatory model involved in the ethnographic interviewing process.* Unpublished paper.

Atkinson, Donald T., Morten, George & Sue, Derald Wing. (1989). *Counseling American minorities: A cross cultural perspective.* Dubuque, IA: William C. Brown.

Basso, Keith. (1970). To give up on words: Silence in Western culture. *South-Western Journal of Anthropology, 26*(3), 213–228.

Crystal, David. (1989). Asian Americans and the myth of the model minority. *Social Casework, 70*(7), 405–413.

Green, James W. (1982). *Cultural awareness in the human services.* Englewood Cliffs, NJ: Prentice-Hall.

Ho, Man Keung. (1982). Case Studies. *Practice Digest, 5*(3), 6–7.

Kagle, Jill Doner. (1988). Overcoming "person-al" errors in assessment. *ARETE, 13*(2), 35–40.

Kenmore, Thomas K. (1987). Negotiating with clients: A study of clinical practice experience. *Social Service Review, 61*(1), 132–143.

Kleinman, Arthur. (1988). *Rethinking psychiatry.* New York: The Free Press.

Kleinman, Arthur, Eisenberg, Leon, & Good, Byron. (1978). Culture, illness and care: Clinical lessons from anthropologic and cross-cultural research. *Annals of Internal Medicine, 88*(2), 251–258.

LaFromboise, Theresa D., & Dixon, David N. (1981). American Indian perception of trustworthiness in a counseling interview. *Journal of Counseling Psychology, 28*(2), 135–139.

Lantz, Jim, & Pegram, Mary. (1989). Cross cultural curative factors and clinical social work. *Journal of Independent Social Work, 4*(1), 55–68.

Leigh, James W. (1985). The ethnically competent social worker. In Joan Laird and Ann Hartman (Eds.), *A handbook of child welfare* (pp. 449–459). New York: The Free Press.

Levine, Elaine, & Padilla, Amado. (1980). *Crossing cultures in therapy: Pluralistic counseling for Hispanics.* Monterey, CA: Brooks/Cole.

Levinson, Daniel J., John Merrifield, & Berg, Kenneth. (1967). Becoming a patient. *Archives of General Psychiatry, 17,* 385–406.

Lewis, Ronald. (1985). Cultural perspectives on treatment modalities with Native Americans. In Martin Bloom (Ed.), *Life span development,* (2nd ed.) (pp. 458–464). New York: Macmillan.

Lewis, Thomas. (1974). An Indian healer's preventive medicine procedures. *Hospital and Community Psychiatry, 25*(2), 94–95.

Maluccio, Anthony N., & Marlow, Wilma D. (1974). The case for contract. *Social Work, 19*(1), 28–36.

Meyer, Carel. (1985). The institutional context of child welfare. In Joan Laird and Ann Hartman (Eds.). *A handbook of child welfare (pp. 110–115). New York: The Free Press.*

Perlman, Helen Harris. (1957). *Social casework: A problem solving process.* Chicago: University of Chicago Press.

Rodwell, M. K. (1987). Naturalistic inquiry: An alternate model for social work assessment. *Social Service Review, 62*(2), 231–246.

Rojek, Chris, & Collins, Stewart A. (1987). "Contract or con trick. *British Journal of Social Work, 17*(2), 199–211.

Seabury, Brett. (1979). Negotiating sound contracts with clients. *Public Welfare, 37*(2), 33–38.

———. (1985). The beginning phrase: Engagement, initial assessment, and contracting. In Joan Laird and Ann Hartman (Eds.), *A handbook of child welfare* (pp. 355–359). New York: The Free Press.

Shriver, Joe M. (1995). *Human behavior and the social environment.* Boston: Allyn and Bacon.

Whittaker, James K., & Tracy, Elizabeth M. (1989). *Social treatment.* New York: A. DeGruyter.

Code of Ethics, The National Association of Social Workers

OVERVIEW

The *NASW Code of Ethics* is intended to serve as a guide to the everyday professional conduct of social workers. This *Code* includes four sections. The first section, "Preamble," summarizes the social work profession's mission and core values. The second section, "Purpose of the *NASW Code of Ethics*," provides an overview of the *Code's* main functions and a brief guide for dealing with ethical issues or dilemmas in social work practice. The third section, "Ethical Principles," presents broad ethical principles, based on social work's core values, that inform social work practice. The final section, "Ethical Standards," includes specific ethical standards to guide social workers' conduct and to provide a basis for adjudication.

PREAMBLE

The primary mission of the social work profession is to enhance human well-being and help meet the basic human needs of all people, with particular attention to the needs and empowerment of people who are vulnerable, oppressed, and living in poverty. A historic and defining feature of social work is the profession's focus on individual well-being in a social context and the well-being of society. Fundamental to social work is attention to the environmental forces that create, contribute to, and address problems in living.

Social workers promote social justice and social change with and on behalf of clients. "Clients" is used inclusively to refer to individuals, families, groups, organizations, and communities. Social workers are sensitive to cultural and ethnic diversity and strive to end discrimination, oppression, poverty, and other forms of social injustice. These activities may be in the form of direct practice, community organizing, supervision, consultation, administration, advocacy, social and political action, policy development and implementation, education, and research and evaluation. Social workers seek to enhance the capacity of people to address their own needs. Social workers also seek to promote the responsiveness of organizations, communities, and other social institutions to individuals' needs and social problems.

The mission of the social work profession is rooted in a set of core values. These core values, embraced by social workers throughout the profession's history, are the foundation of social work's unique purpose and perspective.

- service
- social justice
- dignity and worth of the person
- importance of human relationships
- integrity
- competence

This constellation of core values reflects what is unique to the social work profession. Core values, and the principles that flow from them, must be balanced within the context and complexity of the human experience.

PURPOSE OF THE *NASW CODE OF ETHICS*

Professional ethics are the core of social work. The profession has an obligation to articulate its basic values, ethical principles, and ethical standards. The *NASW Code of Ethics* sets forth these values, principles, and standards to guide social workers' conduct. The *Code* is relevant to all social workers and social work students, regardless of their professional functions, the settings in which they work, or the populations they serve.

The *NASW Code of Ethics* serves six purposes:

1. The *Code* identifies core values on which social work's mission is based.
2. The *Code* summarizes broad ethical principles that reflect the professions' core values and establishes a set of specific ethical standards that should be used to guide social work practice.
3. The *Code* is designed to help social workers identify relevant considerations when professional obligations conflict or ethical uncertainties arise.

4. The *Code* provides ethical standards to which the general public can hold the social work profession accountable.
5. The *Code* socializes practitioners new to the field to social work's mission, values, ethical principles, and ethical standards.
6. The *Code* articulates standards that the social work profession itself can use to assess whether social workers have engaged in unethical conduct. NASW has formal procedures to adjudicate ethics complaints filed against its members.[1] In subscribing to this *Code*, social workers are required to cooperate in its implementation, participate in NASW adjudication proceedings, and abide by any NASW disciplinary rulings or sanctions based on it.

The *Code* offers a set of values, principles, and standards to guide decision making and conduct when ethical issues arise. It does not provide a set of rules that prescribe how social workers should act in all situations. Specific applications of the *Code* must take into account the context in which it is being considered and the possibility of conflicts among the *Code*'s values, principles, and standards. Ethical responsibilities flow from all human relationships, from the personal and familial to the social and professional.

Further, the *NASW Code of Ethics* does not specify which values, principles, and standards are the most important and ought to outweigh others in instances when they conflict. Reasonable differences of opinion can and do exist among social workers with respect to the ways in which values, ethical principles, and ethical standards should be rank ordered when they conflict. Ethical decision making in a given situation must apply the informed judgment of the individual social worker and should also consider how the issues would be judged in a peer review process where the ethical standards of the profession would be applied.

Ethical decision making is a process. There are many instances in social work where simple answers are not available to resolve complex ethical issues. Social workers should take into consideration all the values, principles, and standards in this *Code* that are relevant to any situation in which ethical judgment is warranted. Social workers' decisions and actions should be consistent with the spirit a well as the letter of this *Code*.

In addition to this *Code*, there are many other sources of information about ethical thinking that may be useful. Social workers should consider ethical theory and principles generally, social work theory and research, laws, regulations, agency policies, and other relevant codes of ethics, recognizing that among codes of ethics social workers should consider the *NASW Code of Ethics* as their primary source. Social workers should also be aware of

---

[1] For information on NASW adjudication procedures, see NASW *Procedures for the Adjudication of Grievances.*

the impact on ethical decision making of their clients' and their own personal values and cultural and religious beliefs and practices. They should be aware of any conflicts between personal and professional values and deal with them responsibly. For additional guidance social workers should consider the relevant literature on professional ethics and ethical decision making and seek appropriate consultation when faced with ethical dilemmas. This may involve consultation with an agency-based or social work organization's ethics committee, a regulatory body, knowledgeable colleagues, supervisors, or legal counsel.

Instances may arise when social workers' ethical obligations conflict with agency policies or relevant laws and regulations. When such conflicts occur, social workers must make a responsible effort to resolve the conflict in a manner that is consistent with the values, principles, and standards expressed in this *Code*. If a reasonable resolution of the conflict does not appear possible, social workers should seek proper consultation before making a decision.

The NASW Code of Ethics is to be used by NASW and by individuals, agencies, organizations, and bodies (such as licensing and regulatory boards, professional liability insurance providers, courts of law, agency boards of directors, government agencies, and other professional groups) that choose to adopt it or use it as a frame of reference. Violation of standards in this *Code* does not automatically imply legal liability or violation of the law. Such determination can only be made in the context of legal and judicial proceedings. Alleged violations of the *Code* would be subject to a peer review process. Such processes are generally separate from legal or administrative procedures and insulated from legal review or proceedings to allow the profession to counsel and discipline its own members.

A code of ethics cannot guarantee ethical behavior. Moreover, a code of ethics cannot resolve all ethical issues or disputes or capture the richness and complexity involved in striving to make responsible choices within a moral community. Rather, a code of ethics sets forth values, ethical principles, and ethical standards to which professionals aspire and by which their actions can be judged. Social workers' ethical behavior should result from their personal commitment to engage in ethical practice. The *NASW Code of Ethics* reflects the commitment of all social workers to uphold the profession's values and to act ethically. Principles and standards must be applied by individuals of good character who discern moral questions and, in good faith, seek to make reliable ethical decisions.

ETHICAL PRINCIPLES

The following broad ethical principles are based on social work's core values of service, social justice, dignity and worth of the person, importance of human relationships, integrity, and competence, These principles set forth ideals to which all social workers should aspire.

Value: *Service*

Ethical Principle: *Social workers' primary goal is to help people in need and to address social problems.*

Social workers elevate service to others above self-interest. Social workers draw on their knowledge, values, and skills to help people in need and to address social problems. Social workers are encouraged to volunteer some portion of their professional skills with no expectation of significant financial return (pro bono service).

Value: *Social Justice*

Ethical Principle: *Social workers challenge social injustice.*

Social workers pursue social change, particularly with and on behalf of vulnerable and oppressed individuals and groups of people. Social workers' social change efforts are focused primarily on issues of poverty, unemployment, discrimination, and other forms of social injustice. These activities seek to promote sensitivity to and knowledge about oppression and cultural and ethnic diversity. Social workers strive to ensure access to needed information, services, and resources; equality of opportunity; and meaningful participation in decision making for all people.

Value: *Dignity and Worth of the Person*

Ethical Principle: *Social workers respect the inherent dignity and worth of the person.*

Social workers treat each person in a caring and respectful fashion, mindful of individual differences and cultural and ethnic diversity. Social workers promote clients' socially responsible self-determination. Social workers seek to enhance clients' capacity and opportunity to change and to address their own needs. Social workers are cognizant of their dual responsibility to clients and to the broader society. They seek to resolve conflicts between clients' interests and the broader society's interests in a socially responsible manner consistent with the values, ethical principles, and ethical standards of the profession.

Value: *Importance of Human Relationships*

Ethical Principle: *Social workers recognize the central importance of human relationships.*

Social workers understand that relationships between and among people are an important vehicle for change. Social workers engage people as partners in the helping process. Social workers seek to strengthen relationships among people in a purposeful effort to promote, restore, maintain, and enhance the well-being of individuals, families, social groups, organizations, and communities.

Value: *Integrity*

Ethical Principle: *Social workers behave in a trustworthy manner.*

Social workers are continually aware of the profession's mission, values, ethical principles, and ethical standards and practice in a manner consistent with them. Social workers act honestly and responsibly and promote ethical practices on the part of the organizations with which they are affiliated.

Value: *Competence*

Ethical Principle: *Social workers practice within their areas of competence and develop and enhance their professional expertise.*

Social workers continually strive to increase their professional knowledge and skills and to apply them in practice. Social workers should aspire to contribute to the knowledge base of the profession.

ETHICAL STANDARDS

The following ethical standards are relevant to the professional activities of all social workers. These standards concern (1) social workers' ethical responsibilities to clients, (2) social workers' ethical responsibilities to colleagues, (3) social workers' ethical responsibilities in practice settings, (4) social workers' ethical responsibilities as professionals, (5) social workers' ethical responsibilities to the social work profession, and (6) social workers' ethical responsibilities to the broader society.

Some of the standards that follow are enforceable guidelines for professional conduct, and some are aspirational. The extent to which each standard is enforceable is a matter of professional judgment to be exercised by those responsible for reviewing alleged violations of ethical standards.

1. Social Workers' Ethical Responsibilities to Clients

1.01 Commitment to Clients
Social workers' primary responsibility is to promote the well-being of clients. In general, client's interests are primary. However, social workers'

responsibility to the larger society or specific legal obligations may on limited occasions supersede the loyalty owed clients, and clients should be so advised. (Examples include when a social worker is required by law to report that a client has abused a child or has threatened to harm self or others.)

1.02 Self-Determination

Social workers respect and promote the right of clients to self-determination and assist clients in their efforts to identify and clarify their goals. Social workers may limit clients' right to self-determination when, in the social workers' professional judgment, clients' actions or potential actions pose a serious, foreseeable, and imminent risk to themselves or others.

1.03 Informed Consent

(a) Social workers should provide services to clients only in the context of professional relationships based, when appropriate, on valid informed consent. Social workers should use clear and understandable language to inform clients of the purpose of the services, risks related to the services, limits to service because of the requirements of a third-party payer, relevant costs, reasonable alternatives, clients' right to refuse or withdraw consent, and the time frame covered by the consent. Social workers should provide clients with an opportunity to ask questions.

(b) In instances when clients are not literate or have difficulty understanding the primary language used in the practice setting, social workers should take steps to ensure clients' comprehension. This may include providing clients with a detailed verbal explanation or arranging for a qualified interpreter or translator whenever possible.

(c) In instances when clients lack the capacity to provide informed consent, social workers should protect clients' interests by seeking permission from an appropriate third party, informing clients consistent with the clients' level of understanding. In such instances social workers should seek to ensure that the third party acts in a manner consistent with clients' wishes and interests. Social workers should take reasonable steps to enhance such clients' ability to give informed consent.

(d) In instances when clients are receiving services involuntarily, social workers should provide information about the nature and extent of services and about the extent of clients' right to refuse service.

(e) Social workers who provide services via electronic media (such as computer, telephone, radio, and television) should inform recipients of the limitations and risks associated with such services.

(f) Social workers should obtain clients' informed consent before audiotaping or videotaping clients or permitting observation of services to clients by a third party.

1.04 Competence

(a) Social workers should provide services and represent themselves as competent only within the boundaries of their education, training, license, certification, consultation received, supervised experience, or other relevant professional experience.

(b) Social workers should provide services in substantive areas or use intervention techniques or approaches that are new to them only after engaging in appropriate study, training, consultation, and supervision from people who are competent in those interventions or techniques.

(c) When generally recognized standards do not exist with respect to an emerging area of practice, social workers should exercise careful judgment and take responsible steps (including appropriate education, research, training, consultation, and supervision) to ensure the competence of their work and to protect clients from harm.

1.05 Cultural Competence and Diversity

(a) Social workers should understand culture and its function in human behavior and society, recognizing the strengths that exist in all cultures.

(b) Social workers should have a knowledge base of their clients' cultures and be able to demonstrate competence in the provision of services that are sensitive to clients' cultures and to differences among people and cultural groups.

(c) Social workers should obtain education about and seek to understand the nature of social diversity and oppression with respect to race, ethnicity, national origin, color, sex, sexual orientation, age, marital status, political belief, religion, and mental or physical disability.

1.06 Conflicts of Interest

(a) Social workers should be alert to and avoid conflicts of interest that interfere with the exercise of professional discretion and impartial judgment. Social workers should inform clients when a real or potential conflict of interest arises and take reasonable steps to resolve the issue in a manner that makes the clients' interests primary and protects clients' interests to the greatest extent possible. In some cases, protecting clients' interests may require termination of the professional relationship with proper referral of the client.

(b) Social workers should not take unfair advantage of any professional relationship or exploit others to further their personal, religious, political, or business interests.

(c) Social workers should not engage in dual or multiple relationships with clients or former clients in which there is a risk of exploitation or potential harm to the client. In instances when dual or multiple relationships are unavoidable, social workers should take steps to protect clients and are responsible for setting clear, appropriate, and culturally sensitive boundaries. (Dual or multiple relationships occur when social workers relate to clients in more than one relationship, whether professional, social, or business. Dual or multiple relationships can occur simultaneously or consecutively.)

(d) When social workers provide services to two or more people who have a relationship with each other (for example, couples, family members), social workers should clarify with all parties which individuals will be considered clients and the nature of social workers' professional obligations to the various individuals who are receiving services. Social workers who anticipate a conflict of interest among the individuals receiving services or who anticipate having to perform in potentially conflicting roles (for example, when a social worker is asked to testify in a child custody dispute or divorce proceedings involving clients) should clarify their role with the parties involved and take appropriate action to minimize any conflict of interest.

1.07 Privacy and Confidentiality

(a) Social workers should respect clients' right to privacy. Social workers should not solicit private information from clients unless it is essential to providing services or conducting social work evaluation or research. Once private information is shared, standards of confidentiality apply.

(b) Social workers may disclose confidential information when appropriate with valid consent from a client or a person legally authorized to consent on behalf of a client.

(c) Social workers should protect the confidentiality of all information obtained in the course of professional service, except for compelling professional reasons. The general expectation that social workers will keep information confidential does not apply when disclosure is necessary to prevent serious, foreseeable, and imminent harm to a client or other identifiable person or when laws or regulations require disclosure without a client's consent. In all instances, social workers should disclose the least amount of confidential information necessary to achieve the desired purpose; only information that is directly relevant to the purpose for which the disclosure is made should be revealed.

(d) Social workers should inform clients, to the extent possible, about the disclosure of confidential information and the potential consequences, when feasible before the disclosure is made. This applies whether social workers disclose confidential information on the basis of a legal requirement or client consent.

(e) Social workers should discuss with clients and other interested parties the nature of confidentiality and limitations of clients' right to confidentiality. Social workers should review with clients circumstances where confidential information may be requested and where disclosure of confidential information may be legally required. This discussion should occur as soon as possible in the social worker–client relationship and as needed throughout the course of the relationship.

(f) When social workers provide counseling services to families, couples, or groups, social workers should seek agreement among the parties involved concerning each individual's right to confidentiality and obligation to preserve the confidentiality of information shared by others. Social workers should inform participants in family, couples, or group counseling that social workers cannot guarantee that all participants will honor such agreements.

(g) Social workers should inform clients involved in family, couples, marital, or group counseling of the social worker's, employer's, and agency's policy concerning the social worker's disclosure of confidential information among the parties involved in the counseling.

(h) Social workers should not disclose confidential information to third-party payers unless clients have authorized such disclosure.

(i) Social workers should not discuss confidential information in any setting unless privacy can be ensured. Social workers should not discuss confidential information in public or semipublic areas such as hallways, waiting rooms, elevators, and restaurants.

(j) Social workers should protect the confidentiality of clients during legal proceedings to the extent permitted by law. When a court of law or other legally authorized body orders social workers to disclose confidential or privileged information without a client's consent and such disclosure could cause harm to the client, social workers should request that the court withdraw the order or limit the order as narrowly as possible or maintain the records under seal, unavailable for public inspection.

(k) Social workers should protect the confidentiality of clients when responding to requests from members of the media.

(l) Social workers should protect the confidentiality of clients' written and electronic records and other sensitive information. Social workers should take reasonable steps to ensure that clients' records are stored in a secure location and that clients' records are not available to others who are not authorized to have access.

(m) Social workers should take precautions to ensure and maintain the confidentiality of information transmitted to other parties through the use of computers, electronic mail, facsimile machines, telephones and telephone answering machines, and other electronic or computer technology. Disclosure of identifying information should be avoided whenever possible.

(n) Social workers should transfer or dispose of client's records in a manner that protects clients' confidentiality and is consistent with state statutes governing records and social work licensure.

(o) Social workers should take reasonable precautions to protect client confidentiality in the event of the social worker's termination of practice, incapacitation, or death.

(p) Social workers should not disclose identifying information when discussing clients for teaching or training purposes unless the client has consented to disclosure of confidential information.

(q) Social workers should not disclose identifying information when discussing clients with consultants unless the client has consented to disclosure of confidential information or there is a compelling need for such disclosure.

(r) Social workers should protect the confidentiality of deceased clients consistent with the preceding standards.

1.08 Access to Records

(a) Social workers should provide clients with reasonable access to records concerning the clients. Social workers who are concerned that clients' access to their records could cause serious misunderstanding or harm to the client should provide assistance in interpreting the records and consultation with the client regarding the records. Social workers should limit the clients' access to their records, or portions of their records, only in exceptional circumstances when there is compelling evidence that such access would cause harm to the client. Both clients' requests and the rationale for withholding some or all of the record should be documented in the clients' files.

(b) When providing clients with access to their records, social workers should take steps to protect the confidentiality of other individuals identified or discussed in such records.

1.09 Sexual Relationships

(a) Social workers should under no circumstances engage in sexual activities or sexual contact with current clients, whether such contact is consensual or forced.

(b) Social workers should not engage in sexual activities or sexual contact with client relatives or other individuals with whom clients maintain a close personal relationship when there is a risk of exploitation or potential harm to the client. Sexual activity or sexual contact with the clients' relatives or other individuals with whom clients maintain a personal relationship has the potential to be harmful to the client and may make it difficult for the social worker and client to maintain appropriate professional boundaries. Social workers—not their clients, their clients' relatives, or other individuals with whom the client maintains a personal relationship—assume the full burden for setting clear, appropriate, and culturally sensitive boundaries.

(c) Social workers should not engage in sexual activities or sexual contact with former clients because of the potential for harm to the client. If social workers engage in conduct contrary to this prohibition or claim that an exception to this prohibition is warranted because of extraordinary circumstances, it is social workers—not their clients—who assume the full burden of demonstrating that the former client has not been exploited, coerced, or manipulated, intentionally or unintentionally.

(d) Social workers should not provide clinical services to individuals with whom they have had a prior sexual relationship. Providing clinical services to a former sexual partner has the potential to be harmful to the individual and is likely to make it difficult for the social worker and individual to maintain appropriate professional boundaries.

1.10 Physical Contact
Social workers should not engage in physical contact with clients when there is a possibility of psychological harm to the client as a result of the contact (such as cradling or caressing clients). Social workers who engage in appropriate physical contact with clients are responsible for setting clear, appropriate, and culturally sensitive boundaries that govern such physical contact.

1.11 Sexual Harassment
Social workers should not sexually harass clients. Sexual harassment includes sexual advances, sexual solicitation, requests for sexual favors, and other verbal or physical conduct of a sexual nature.

1.12 Derogatory Language
Social workers should not use derogatory language in their written or verbal communications to or about clients. Social workers should use accurate and respectful language in all communications to and about clients.

1.13 Payment for Services
(a) When setting fees, social workers should ensure that the fees are fair, reasonable, and commensurate with the service performed. Consideration should be given to clients' ability to pay.

(b) Social workers should avoid accepting goods or services from clients as payment for professional services. Bartering arrangements, particularly involving services, create the potential for conflicts of interest, exploitation, and inappropriate boundaries in social workers' relationships with clients. Social workers should explore and may participate in bartering only in very limited circumstances when it can be demonstrated that such arrangements are an accepted practice among professionals in the local community, considered to be essential for the provision of services, negotiated without coercion, and entered into at the client's initiative and with the client's informed consent. Social workers who accept goods or services from clients as payment for professional services assume the full burden of demonstrating that this arrangement will not be detrimental to the client or the professional relationship.

(c) Social workers should not solicit a private fee or other remuneration for providing services to clients who are entitled to such available services through the social workers' employer or agency.

1.14 Clients Who Lack Decision-Making Capacity

When social workers act on behalf of clients who lack the capacity to make informed decisions, social workers should take reasonable steps to safeguard the interests and rights of those clients.

1.15 Interruption of Services

Social workers should make reasonable efforts to ensure continuity of services in the event that services are interrupted by factors such as unavailability, relocation, illness, disability, or death.

1.16 Termination of Services

(a) Social workers should terminate services to clients and professional relationships with them when such services and relationships are no longer required or no longer serve the clients' needs or interests.

(b) Social workers should take reasonable steps to avoid abandoning clients who are in need of services. Social workers should withdraw services precipitously only under unusual circumstances, giving careful consideration to all factors in the situation and taking care to minimize possible adverse effects. Social workers should assist in making appropriate arrangements for continuation of services when necessary.

(c) Social workers in fee-for-service settings may terminate services to clients who are not paying an overdue balance if the financial contractual arrangements have been made clear to the client, if the client does not pose an imminent danger to self or others, and if the clinical and other consequences of the current nonpayment have been addressed and discussed with the client.

(d) Social workers should not terminate services to pursue a social, financial, or sexual relationship with a client.

(e) Social workers who anticipate the termination or interruption of services to clients should notify clients promptly and seek the transfer, referral, or continuation of services in relation to the clients' needs and preferences.

(f) Social workers who are leaving an employment setting should inform clients of appropriate options for the continuation of services and of the benefits and risks of options.

2. Social Workers' Ethical Responsibilities to Colleagues

2.01. Respect
(a) Social workers should treat colleagues with respect and should represent accurately and fairly the qualifications, views, and obligations of colleagues.

(b) Social workers should avoid unwarranted negative criticism of colleagues in communications with clients or with other professionals. Unwarranted negative criticism may include demeaning comments that refer to colleagues' level of competence or to individuals' attributes such as race, ethnicity, national origin, color, sex, sexual orientation, age, marital status, political belief, religion, and mental or physical disability.

(c) Social workers should cooperate with social work colleagues and with colleagues of other professions when such cooperation serves the well-being of clients.

2.02 Confidentiality
Social workers should respect confidential information shared by colleagues in the course of their professional relationships and transactions. Social workers should ensure that such colleagues understand social workers' obligation to respect confidentiality and any exceptions related to it.

2.03 Interdisciplinary Collaboration
(a) Social workers who are members of an interdisciplinary team should participate in and contribute to decisions that affect the well-being of clients by drawing on the perspectives, values, and experiences of the social work profession. Professional and ethical obligations of the interdisciplinary team as a whole and of its individual members should be clearly established.

(b) Social workers for whom a team decision raises ethical concerns should attempt to resolve the disagreement through appropriate channels. If the disagreement cannot be resolved, social workers should pursue other avenues to address their concerns consistent with client well-being.

2.04 Disputes Involving Colleagues
(a) Social workers should not take advantage of a dispute between a colleague and an employer to obtain a position or otherwise advance the social worker's own interests.

(b) Social workers should not exploit clients in disputes with colleagues or engage clients in any inappropriate discussion of conflicts between social workers and their colleagues.

2.05 Consultation

(a) Social workers should seek the advise and counsel of colleagues whenever such consultation is in the best interests of clients.

(b) Social workers should keep themselves informed about colleagues' areas of expertise and competencies. Social workers should seek consultation only from colleagues who have demonstrated knowledge, expertise, and competence related to the subject of the consultation.

(c) When consulting with colleagues about clients, social workers should disclose the least amount of information necessary to achieve the purposes of the consultation.

2.06 Referral for Services

(a) Social workers should refer clients to other professionals when the other professionals' specialized knowledge or expertise is needed to serve clients fully or when social workers believe that they are not being effective or making reasonable progress with clients and that additional service is required.

(b) Social workers who refer clients to other professionals should take appropriate steps to facilitate an orderly transfer of responsibility. Social workers who refer clients to other professionals should disclose, with clients' consent, all pertinent information to the new service providers.

(c) Social workers are prohibited from giving or receiving payment for a referral when no professional service is provided by the referring social worker.

2.07 Sexual Relationships

(a) Social workers who function as supervisors or educators should not engage in sexual activities or contacts with supervisees, students, trainees, or other colleagues over whom they exercise professional authority.

(b) Social workers should avoid engaging in sexual relationships with colleagues when there is potential for a conflict of interest. Social workers who become involved in, or anticipate becoming involved in, a sexual relationship with a colleague have a duty to transfer professional responsibilities, when necessary, to avoid conflict of interest.

2.08 Sexual Harassment

Social workers should not sexually harass supervisees, students, trainees, or colleagues. Sexual harassment includes sexual advances, sexual solicitation, requests for sexual favors, and other verbal or physical conduct of a sexual nature.

2.09   Impairment of Colleagues

(a) Social workers who have direct knowledge of a social work colleague's impairment that is due to personal problems, psychosocial distress, substance abuse, or mental health difficulties and that interferes with practice effectiveness should consult with that colleague when feasible and assist the colleague in taking remedial action.

(b) Social workers who believe that a social work colleague's impairment interferes with practice effectiveness and that the colleague has not taken adequate steps to address the impairment should take action through appropriate channels established by employers, agencies, NASW, licensing and regulatory bodies, and other professional organizations.

2.10   Incompetence of Colleagues

(a) Social workers who have direct knowledge of a social work colleague's incompetence should consult with that colleague when feasible and assist the colleague in taking remedial action.

(b) Social workers who believe that a social work colleague is incompetent and has not taken adequate steps to address the incompetence should take action through appropriate channels established by employers, agencies, NASW, licensing and regulatory bodies, and other professional organizations.

2.11   Unethical Conduct of Colleagues

(a) Social workers should take adequate measures to discourage, prevent, expose, and correct the unethical conduct of colleagues.

(b) Social workers should be knowledgeable about established policies and procedures for handling concerns about colleagues' unethical behavior. Social workers should be familiar with national, state, and local procedures for handling ethics complaints. These include policies and procedures created by NASW, licensing and regulatory bodies, employers, agencies, and other professional organizations.

(c) Social workers who believe that a colleague has acted unethically should seek resolution by discussing their concerns with the colleague when feasible and when such discussion is likely to be productive.

(d) When necessary, social workers who believe that a colleague has acted unethically should take action through appropriate formal channels (such as contacting a state licensing board or regulatory body, an NASW committee on inquiry or other professional ethics committees).

(e) Social workers should defend and assist colleagues who are unjustly charged with unethical conduct.

3. Social Workers' Ethical Responsibilities in Practice Settings

3.01 Supervision and Consultation

(a) Social workers who provide supervision or consultation should have the necessary knowledge and skill to supervise or consult appropriately, and should do so only within their areas of knowledge and competence.

(b) Social workers who provide supervision or consultation are responsible for setting clear, appropriate, and culturally sensitive boundaries.

(c) Social workers should not engage in any dual or multiple relationships with supervisees in which there is a risk of exploitation or potential harm to the supervisee.

(d) Social workers who provide supervision should evaluate supervisees' performance in a manner that is fair and respectful.

3.02 Education and Training

(a) Social workers who function as educators, field instructors for students, or trainers should provide instruction only within their areas of knowledge and competence and should provide instruction based on the most current information and knowledge available in the profession.

(b) Social workers who function as educators or field instructors for students should evaluate students' performance in a manner that is fair and respectful.

(c) Social workers who function as educators or field instructors for students should take reasonable steps to ensure that clients are routinely informed when services are being provided by students.

(d) Social workers who function as educators or field instructors for students should not engage in any dual or multiple relationships with students in which there is a risk of exploitation or potential harm to the student. Social work educators or field instructors are responsible for setting clear, appropriate, and culturally sensitive boundaries.

3.03 Performance Evaluation

Social workers who have responsibility for evaluating the performance of others should fulfill such responsibility in a fair and considerate manner and on the basis of clearly stated criteria.

3.04 Client Records

(a) Social workers should take reasonable steps to ensure that documentation in records is accurate and reflects the services provided.

(b) Social workers should include sufficient and timely documentation in records to facilitate the delivery of services and to ensure continuity of services provided to clients in the future.

(c) Social workers' documentation should protect clients' privacy to the extent that is possible and appropriate and should include only information that is directly relevant to the delivery of services.

(d) Social workers should store records following the termination of services to ensure reasonable future access. Records should be maintained for the number of years required by state statutes or relevant contracts.

3.05 Billing

Social workers should establish and maintain billing practices that accurately reflect the nature and extent of services provided and that identify who provided the service in the practice setting.

3.06 Client Transfer

(a) When an individual who is receiving services from another agency or colleague contacts a social worker for services, the social worker should carefully consider the client's needs before agreeing to provide services. To minimize possible confusion and conflict, social workers should discuss with potential clients the nature of the clients' current relationship with the other service providers and the implications, including possible benefits or risks, of entering into a relationship with a new service provider.

(b) If a new client has been served by another agency or colleague, social workers should discuss with the client whether consultation with the previous service provider is in the client's best interest.

3.07 Administration

(a) Social work administrators should advocate within and outside their agencies for adequate resources to meet clients' needs.

(b) Social workers should advocate for resource allocation procedures that are open and fair. When not all clients' needs can be met, an allocation procedure should be developed that is nondiscriminatory and based on appropriate and consistently applied principles.

(c) Social workers who are administrators should take reasonable steps to ensure that adequate agency or organizational resources are available to provide appropriate staff supervision.

(d) Social work administrators should take reasonable steps to ensure that the working environment for which they are responsible is consistent with the *NASW Code of Ethics*. Social work administrators should take reasonable steps to eliminate any conditions in their organizations that violate, interfere with, or discourage compliance with the *Code*.

3.08 Continuing Education and Staff Development

(a) Social work administrators and supervisors should take reasonable steps to provide or arrange for continuing education and staff development for all staff for whom they are responsible. Continuing education and staff development should address current knowledge and energizing developments related to social work practice and ethics.

3.09 Commitments to Employers

(a) Social workers generally should adhere to commitments made to employers and employing organizations.

(b) Social workers should work to improve employing agencies' policies and procedures and the efficiency and effectiveness of their services.

(c) Social workers should take reasonable steps to ensure that employers are aware of social workers' ethical obligations as set forth in the *NASW Code of Ethics* and of the implications of those obligations for social work practice.

(d) Social workers should not allow an employing organization's policies, procedures, regulations. or administrative orders to interfere with their ethical practice of social work. Social workers should take reasonable steps to ensure that their employing organizations' practices are consistent with the *NASW Code of Ethics*.

(e) Social workers should act to prevent and eliminate discrimination in the employing organization's work assignments and in its employment policies and practices.

(f) Social workers should accept employment or arrange student field placements only in organizations that exercise fair personnel practices.

(g) Social workers should be diligent stewards of the resources of their employing organizations, wisely conserving funds where appropriate and never misappropriating funds or using them for unintended purposes.

3.10 Labor-Management Disputes

(a) Social workers may engage in organized action, including the formation of and participation in labor unions, to improve services to clients and working conditions.

(b) The actions of social workers who are involved in labor-management disputes, job actions, or labor strikes should be guided by the profession's values, ethical principles, and ethical standards. Reasonable differences of opinion exist among social workers concerning their primary obligations as professionals during an actual or threatened labor strike or job action. Social workers should carefully examine relevant issues and their possible impact on clients before deciding on a course of action.

4. Social Workers' Ethical Responsibilities as Professionals

4.01 Competence

(a) Social workers should accept responsibility or employment only on the basis of existing competence or the intention to acquire the necessary competence.

(b) Social workers should strive to become and remain proficient in professional practice and the performance of professional functions. Social workers should critically examine and keep current with emerging knowledge relevant to social work. Social workers should routinely review the professional literature and participate in continuing education relevant to social work practice and social work ethics.

(c) Social workers should base practice on recognized knowledge, including empirically based knowledge, relevant to social work practice and social work ethics.

4.02 Discrimination

Social workers should not practice, condone, facilitate, or collaborate with any form of discrimination on the basis of race, ethnicity, national origin, color, sex, sexual orientation, age, marital status, political belief, religion, or mental or physical disability.

4.03 Private Conduct

Social workers should not permit their private conduct to interfere with their ability to fulfill their professional responsibilities.

4.04 Dishonesty, Fraud, and Deception

Social workers should not participate in, condone, or be associated with dishonesty, fraud, or deception.

4.05 Impairment

(a) Social workers should not allow their own personal problems, psychosocial distress, legal problems, substance abuse, or mental health difficulties to interfere with their professional judgment and performance or to jeopardize the best interests of people for whom they have a professional responsibility.

(b) Social workers whose personal problems, psychosocial distress, legal problems, substance abuse, or mental health difficulties interfere with their professional judgment and performance should immediately seek consultation and take appropriate remedial action by seeking professional help, making adjustments in workload, terminating practice, or taking any other steps necessary to protect clients and others.

4.06 Misrepresentation

(a) Social workers should make clear distinctions between statements made and actions engaged in as a private individual and as a representative of the social work profession, a professional social work organization, or the social worker's employing agency.

(b) Social workers who speak on behalf of professional social work organizations should accurately represent the official and authorized positions of the organization.

(c) Social workers should ensure that their representations to clients, agencies, and the public of professional qualifications, credentials, education, competence, affiliations, services provided, or results to be achieved are accurate. Social workers should claim only those relevant professional credentials they actually possess and take steps to correct any inaccuracies or misrepresentations of their credentials by others.

4.07 Solicitations

(a) Social workers should not engage in uninvited solicitation of potential clients who, because of their circumstances, are vulnerable to undue influence, manipulation, or coercion.

(b) Social workers should not engage in solicitation of testimonial endorsements (including solicitation of consent to use a client's prior statement as a testimonial endorsement) from current clients or from other people who, because of their particular circumstances, are vulnerable to undue influence.

4.08 Acknowledging Credit

(a) Social workers should take responsibility and credit, including authorship credit, only for work they have actually performed and to which they have contributed.

(b) Social workers should honestly acknowledge the work of and the contributions made by others.

5. Social Workers' Ethical Responsibilities to the Social Work Profession

5.01 Integrity of the Profession

(a) Social workers should work toward the maintenance and promotion of high standards of practice.

(b) Social workers should uphold and advance the values, ethics, knowledge, and mission of the profession. Social workers should protect, enhance, and improve the integrity of the profession through appropriate study and research, active discussion, and responsible criticism of the profession.

(c) Social workers should contribute time and professional expertise to activities that promote respect for the value, integrity, and competence of the social work profession. These activities may include teaching, research, consultation, service, legislative testimony, presentations in the community, and participation in their professional organization.

(d) Social workers should contribute to the knowledge base of social work and share with colleagues their knowledge related to practice, research, and ethics. Social workers should seek to contribute to the profession's literature and to share their knowledge at professional meetings and conferences.

(e) Social workers should act to prevent the unauthorized and unqualified practice of social work.

5.02 Evaluation and Research

(a) Social workers should monitor and evaluate policies, the implementation of programs, and practice interventions.

(b) Social workers should promote and facilitate evaluation and research to contribute to the development of knowledge.

(c) Social workers should critically examine and keep current with emerging knowledge relevant to social work and fully use evaluation and research evidence in their professional practice.

(d) Social workers engaged in evaluation or research should carefully consider possible consequences and should follow guidelines developed for the protection of evaluation and research participants. Appropriate institutional review boards should be consulted.

(e) Social workers engaged in evaluation or research should obtain voluntary and written informed consent from participants when appropriate, without any implied or actual deprivation or penalty for refusal to participate; without undue inducement to participate; and with due regard for participants' well-being, privacy, and dignity. Informed consent should include information about the nature, extent, and duration of the participation requested and disclosure of the risks and benefits of participation in the research.

(f) When evaluation or research participants are incapable of giving informed consent, social workers should provide an appropriate explanation to the participants, obtain the participants' assent to the extent they are able, and obtain written consent from an appropriate agency.

(g) Social workers should never design or conduct evaluation or research that does not use consent procedures, such as certain forms of naturalistic observation and archival research, unless rigorous and responsible review of the research has found it to be justified because of its prospective scientific, educational, or applied value and unless equally effective alternative procedures that do not involve waiver of consent are not feasible.

(h) Social workers should inform participants of their right to withdraw from evaluation and research at any time without penalty.

(i) Social workers should take appropriate steps to ensure that participants in evaluation and research have access to appropriate supportive services.

(j) Social workers engaged in evaluation or research should protect participants from unwarranted physical or mental distress, harm, danger, or deprivation.

(k) Social workers engaged in the evaluation of services should discuss collected information only for professional purposes and only with people professionally concerned with this information.

(l) Social workers engaged in evaluation or research should ensure the anonymity or confidentiality of participants and of the data obtained from them. Social workers should inform participants of any limits of confidentiality, the measures that will be taken to ensure confidentiality, and when any records containing research data will be destroyed.

(m) Social workers who report evaluation and research results should protect participants' confidentiality by omitting identifying information unless proper consent has been obtained authorizing disclosure.

(n) Social workers should report evaluation and research findings accurately. They should not fabricate or falsify results and should take steps to correct any errors later found in published data using standard publication methods.

(o) Social workers engaged in evaluation or research should be alert to and avoid conflicts of interest and dual relationships with participants, should inform participants when a real or potential conflict of interest arises, and should take steps to resolve the issue in a manner that makes participants' interests primary.

(p) Social workers should educate themselves, their students, and their colleagues about responsible research practices.

6. Social Workers' Ethical Responsibilities to the Broader Society

6.01 Social Welfare
Social workers should promote the general welfare of society, from local to global levels, and the development of people, their communities, and their environments. Social workers should advocate for living conditions conducive to the fulfillment of basic human needs and should promote social, economic, political, and cultural values and institutions that are compatible with the realization of social justice.

6.02 Public Participation
Social workers should facilitate informed participation by the public in shaping social policies and institutions.

6.03 Public Emergencies
Social workers should provide appropriate professional services in public emergencies to the greatest extent possible.

6.04 Social and Political Action
(a) Social workers should engage in social and political action that seeks to ensure that all people have equal access to the resources, employment, services, and opportunities they require to meet their basic human needs and to develop fully. Social workers should be aware of the impact of the political arena on practice and should advocate for changes in policy and legislation to improve social conditions in order to meet basic human needs and promote social justice.

(b) Social workers should act to expand choice and opportunity for all people, with special regard for vulnerable, disadvantaged, oppressed, and exploited people and groups.

(c) Social workers should promote conditions that encourage respect for cultural and social diversity within the United States and globally. Social workers should promote policies and practices that demonstrate respect for difference, support the expansion of cultural knowledge and resources, advocate for programs and institutions that demonstrate cultural competence, and promote policies that safeguard the rights of and confirm equity and social justice for all people.

(d) Social workers should act to prevent and eliminate domination of, exploitation of, and discrimination against any person, group, or class on the basis of race, ethnicity, national origin, color, sex, sexual orientation, age, marital status, political belief, religion, or mental or physical disability.

Code of Ethics, National Federation of Societies for Clinical Social Work

I. General Responsibilities of Clinical Social Workers

Clinical social workers maintain high standards of the profession in all of their professional roles. Clinical social workers value professional competence, objectivity, and integrity. They consistently use, and attempt to expand the knowledge upon which practice is based, working to ensure that their services are used appropriately and accepting responsibility for the consequences of their work.

II. Responsibility to Clients

The clinical social worker's responsibility is to the client. Clinical social workers respect the integrity, protect the welfare, and maximize the self-determination of the clients with whom they work.

III. Relationships with Colleagues

Clinical social workers act with integrity in their relationships with colleagues and members of other professions. They know and take into account the traditions, practices, and areas of competence of other professionals and cooperate with them fully for the welfare of clients.

IV. Remuneration

Fees set by clinical social workers are in accord with professional standards that protect the client and the profession.

V. Confidentiality
The safeguarding of the client's right to privacy is a basic responsibility of the clinical social worker. Clinical social workers have a primary obligation to maintain the confidentiality of material that has been transmitted to them in any of their professional roles, including the identity of the client.

VI. Societal and Legal Standards
Clinical social workers show sensible regard for the social codes and ethical expectations in their communities, recognizing that violations of accepted, ethical, and legal standards on their part may compromise the fulfillment of their professional responsibilities or reduce public trust in the professional.

VII. Pursuit of Research and Scholarly Activities
In planning, conducting, and reporting a study, the investigator has the responsibility to make a careful evaluation of its ethical acceptability, taking into account the following additional principles for research with human subjects. To the extent that this appraisal, weighing scientific and humane values, suggests a compromise of any principle, the investigator incurs an increasingly serious obligation to seek advice and to observe stringent safeguards to protect the rights of the research participants.

VIII. Public Statements
Public statements, announcements of services, and promotional activities of clinical social workers serve the purpose of providing sufficient information to aid consumers in making informed judgments and choices. Clinical social workers state accurately, objectively, and without misrepresentation their professional qualifications, affiliations, and functions as well as those of the institutions or organizations with which they or their statements may be associated. They should correct the misrepresentations of others with respect to these matters.

Code of Ethics, National Association of Black Social Workers

In America today, no Black person, except the selfish or irrational, can claim neutrality in the quest for Black liberation nor fail to consider the implications of the events taking place in our society. Given the necessity for committing ourselves to the struggle for freedom, we as Black Americans practicing in the field of social welfare set forth this statement of ideals and guiding principles.

If a sense of community awareness is a precondition to humanitarian acts, then we as Black social workers must use our knowledge of the Black community, our commitments to its self determination and our helping skills for the benefit of Black people as we marshal our expertise to improve the quality of life of Black people. Our activities will be guided by our Black consciousness, our determination to protect the security of the Black community and to serve as advocates to relieve suffering of Black people by any means necessary.

Therefore, as Black social workers we commit ourselves, collectively, to the interests of our Black brethren and as individuals subscribe to the following statements:

- I regard as my primary obligation the welfare of the Black individual, Black family, and Black community and will engage in action for improving social conditions.
- I give precedence to this mission over my personal interests.
- I adopt the concept of a Black extended family and embrace all Black

people as my brothers and sisters, making no distinction between their destiny and my own.

- I hold myself responsible for the quality and extent of service I perform and the quality and extent of service performed by the agency or organization in which I am employed, as it relates to the Black community.
- I accept the responsibility to protect the Black community against unethical and hypocritical practice by any individuals or organizations engaged in social welfare activities.
- I stand ready to supplement my paid or professional advocacy with voluntary service in the Black public interest.
- I will consciously use my skills, and my whole being, as an instrument for social change, with particular attention directed to the establishment of Black social institutions.

Seven Principles for the Culturally Competent Social Worker

The culturally competent social worker is aware that any helping situation must be consistent and consonant with the historical and contemporary culture of the person, family, and community. The culturally competent social worker takes into account the nature of exchange relationships which characterize and give objective and subjective meanings to helping encounters. Healing, helping, and curing are culturally specific activities. Critical images and symbolisms must be shared in the professional encounter. Language used is the outcome of the exchange itself. The culturally contracting person will gain insight as a result of the culturally competent social worker's sensitivity to language which reveals how the person hurts, why they hurt, and from where the hurt comes. It is by these efforts that the culturally competent social worker demonstrates understanding, caring, empathy, and acceptance, and achieves a measure of trust necessary to further the enabling process.

The Seven Principles

1. I accept the fact I have much to learn about others.
2. I have an appreciation of the regional and geographical factors related to people of color and contrasting cultures, how the individual may vary from the generalizations about their regional and geographic group, and how regional groups vary from the total cultural group.

Developed by James Anderson, Gloria Richardson, and James Leigh, 1987.

3. I follow the standard that knowledge is obtained from the person in the situation and add to my learning about the situation from that person before generalizing about the group-specific person.
4. I have the capacity to form relationships with people from contrasting cultures in social, work, and professional relationships.
5. I can engage in a process characterized by mutual respect and conscious effort to reduce power disparities between myself and persons of minority status.
6. I have the ability to obtain culturally relevant information in the professional encounter.
7. I have the ability to enter into a process of mutual exploration, assessment, and treatment with people of contrasting cultures and minority status in society.

GLOSSARY

Cover term: A linguistic label that literally covers a range of meanings and usage of a culture.

Cultural guide or informant: A person who assumes the role of teacher about the culture of which he or she is a member.

Cultural knowledge: The acquired knowledge people use to interpret experience and generate behavior.

Culture: The way a group lives, the ethnic background, the race, the values and norms of behavior, and ways of thinking that are passed down through generations and make the person a member of an identifiable group in society. A myriad of forces that effect every aspect of a person's life and give order to that life.

Descriptors: The information that deepens an understanding of the cover term.

Dyad: Two persons interacting in a process of communication and information exchange.

Ethnic: A group of people who are identified by virtue of a set of values and behaviors adhered to over generations.

Ethnographic summary: A body of information that is written in the words of the cultural guide and made up of cover terms and the descriptors for those cover terms.

Ethnography: The work of describing culture; the benchmark of cultural anthropology; the study of explicit and tacit cultural knowledge.

Global question: An open ended inquiry to discover the why, when, and what of an area that the social worker is interested in learning about.

Interventions: The activities taken or the manifest expression of intentionality or act of coming between the client and the problem or influencing the task of change.

Jargon: Words and phrases use by people that reflect the insider's perspective; specialized vocabulary and idioms of those in the same work, profession, or culture.

Race: A classification of persons based on some identifiable physical characteristics such as hair texture or skin color.

Role: A function assumed by someone.

Stranger: A person who lacks knowledge about the customs, language, values, and norms of behaviors of a culture.

Tacit culture: That part of cultural knowledge that remains outside of awareness but is the basis for automatic responses.

Triad: A group of three associated persons.

BIBLIOGRAPHY

Abad, Vincente, Ramos, Juan, & Boyce, Elizabeth. (1974). A model for delivery of mental health services to Spanish-speaking minorities. *American Journal of Orthopsychiatry, 44*(4), 584–595.

Alcabes, Abraham, & Jones, James A. (1985). Structural determinants of "clienthood." *Social Work, 30*(1), 49–53.

Allen-Agbro, Edree. (1996). Personal communication. May 14.

Anderson, James R. (1989). Personal communication.

Andrews, William L. (Ed.). (1996). *The Oxford Frederick Douglass reader.* New York: Oxford University Press.

Ashby, Marianne. (1990). *What is cultural treatment?* Unpublished manuscript.

Ashby, Marianne, & Leigh, James W. (1990). *The three phases of the explanatory model involved in ethnographic interviewing.* Unpublished paper.

Atkinson, Donald T., Morten, George, & Sue, Derald Wing. (1989). *Counseling American minorities: A cross cultural perspective.* Dubuque, IA: William C. Brown.

Axelson, John A. (1985). *Counseling and development in a multicultural society.* Monterey, CA: Brooks/Cole.

Baldwin, James. (1985). *The evidence of things not seen.* New York: Holt, Rinehart & Winston.

Basso, Keith. (1970). To give up on words: Silence in Western culture. *South Western Journal of Anthropology, 26*(3), 213–228.

Bell, Derrick. (1996). *Gospel choirs.* New York: Basic Books.

Benjamin, Alfred. (1974). *The helping interview.* New York: Houghton Mifflin.

Berman-Rossi, Toby, & Miller, Irving. (1994). African-Americans and the settlement during the late nineteenth and early twentieth centuries. *Social Work with Groups, 17*(3), 7–95.

Berry, Brewton, & Tischler, Harry L. (1978). *Race and ethnic relations.* Boston: Houghton Mifflin.

Bettelheim, Bruno. (1983). *Freud and man's soul.* New York: Knopf.

Boyer, Bryce. (1964). Psychoanalytic insights in working with ethnic minorities. *Social Casework, 45*(8), 519–526.

Brammer, Lawrence M. (1973). *The helping relationship: Process and skills.* Englewood Cliffs, NJ: Prentice Hall.

Breslin, Richard W., Cushner, Kenneth, Cherrie, Craig, & Young, Mahealani. (1986). *International interactions: A practical guide.* Beverly Hills, CA: Sage.

Brewster, David. (1996, March 20). The encumbered self. *Seattle Weekly,* 17–23.

Brown, Luna. (1950). Race as a factor in establishing a casework relationship. *Journal of Social Casework, 32*(3), 91–97.

Burke, Ronald K. (1996). *Frederick Douglass: Crusading orator for human rights.* New York: Garland.

Cecchin, Gianfranco, Lane, Gerry, & Ray, Wendel A. (1994). *The cybernetics of prejudices in the practice of psychotherapy.* London: Karnac.

Chestang, Leon. (1980). Competencies and knowledge in clinical social work: A dual perspective. In Patricia Ewalt (Ed.), *Towards a definition of clinical social work* (pp. 1–22). Washington, DC: National Association of Social Workers.

Chunn, Jay C., Dunston, Patricia J., & Ross-Sheriff, Fariyal (Eds.). (1983). *Mental health and people of color: Curriculum development and change.* Washington, DC: Howard University Press.

Cisneros, Henry. (1988). The demography of a dream. *New Perspectives Quarterly, 5*(2), 36–39.

Cross, Terry, Bazron, Barbara J., Dennis, Karl W., & Isaacs, Mareasa R. (1989). *Towards a culturally competent system of care.* Washington, DC: Georgetown University Child Development Center.

Crystal, David. (1989). Asian Americans and the myths of the model minority. *Social Casework, 70*(7), 405–413.

Cuddihy, John Murray. (1974). *The ordeal of civility.* New York: Basic Books.

Curry, Andrew. (1964). The Negro worker and the White client: A commentary on the treatment relationship. *Social Casework, 45*(3), 131–136.

———. (1973). *Bringing forth forms.* Paradise: CA: Dustbooks.

Dean, John P., Eichorn, Robert L., & Dean, Lois R. (1967). Observation and interviewing. In T. Doby (Ed.), *An introduction to social research* (pp. 274–304). New York: Meredith.

Denzin, Norman K. (1971). The logic of naturalistic inquiry. *Social Forces, 50*(2), 166–182.

deSchweintz, Elizabeth. (1948). *Courtesy: A requirement for the social worker.* Washington, DC: Federal Security Agency, Social Service Administration, Bureau of Public Assistance.

Devore, Wynetta, & Schlesinger, Alfriede. (1981). *Ethnic sensitive social work practice.* St. Louis: C.V. Mosby.

Dieppa, Ismael. (1984). Trends in social work education for minorities. In Barbara W. White (Ed.), *Color in a white society.* Silver Springs, MD: National Association of Social Workers.

Dindia, Kathryn. (1995). Self-disclosure: A sense of balance. *Contemporary Psychology, 40*(1), 17–18.

Dong, Clarene N. (1974). Clinical social work practice. In F. L. Feldman (Ed.), *Social work papers* (pp. 48–59). Los Angeles: University of Southern California.

Draguns, Juris G. (1976). Counseling across cultures: Common themes and distinct approaches. In Paul Pedersen, William J. Lonner, & Juris G. Draguns (Eds.), *Counseling across cultures*. Honolulu, HI: The University of Hawaii Press.

Dubois, William E. B. (1903). *The souls of black folk: Essays and sketches*. Chicago: McClurg.

Ellison, Ralph. (1952). *Invisible man*. New York: Random House.

———. (1964). *Shadow and act*. New York: Random House.

English, Richard. (1984). *The challenge for mental health: Minorities and their world views*. Austin, TX: University of Texas Press.

Fenalson, Anne. (1962). *Essentials of interviewing*. Revised by Grace. B. Ferguson & Arthur Abrahamson. New York: Harper & Row.

Fibush, Esther. (1965). The white worker and the negro client. *Social Casework, 46*(5), 271–277.

Fleming, Robert. (1996). *The wisdom of elders*. New York: Ballantine.

Freimanis, Carolina. (1994). Training bilinguals to interpret in the community. In Richard W. Breslin & Tomoko Yoshida (Eds.), *Improving interactions: Modules for cross-cultural training programs*. Thousand Oaks, CA: Sage.

Garrett, Annette Marie. (1972). *Interviewing: Its principles and methods* (2nd ed.) Revised by Elinor P. Zaki & Margaret Mangold. New York: Family Association of America.

Gallegos, Joseph, & Harris, Anita. (1979). Toward a model for the inclusion of ethnic minority content in doctoral social work education. *Journal of Education for Social Work, 15*(1), 29–35.

Gibbs, Jewell Taylor. (1985). Treatment relationships with black clients: Interpersonal vs. instrumental strategies. In Carel B. Germain (Ed.), *Advances in clinical social work practice* (pp. 184–196). Silver Springs, MD: National Association of Social Workers.

Gil, Rosa M. (1984, May 17). The ethnic patient: Implications for medical social work practice. In *Cross-cultural issues: Impact on social work practice in health care; conference proceedings* (pp. 19–32). New York: Columbia University School of Social Work and Social Work Departments in Harlem, Morristown Memorial, Mt. Sinai, New York Psychiatric Institute, Presbyterian, St. Luke's and Roosevelt Hospitals.

Gomez, Ernesto, & Becker, Roy E. (1985). Comparisons between the perceptions of human service workers and Chicano clients. *Social Thought, 11*(3), 40–48.

Gray, Sylvia Sims, Hartman, Ann, & Saalberg, Ellen S. (1985). *Empowering the black family*. Ann Arbor, MI: University of Michigan School of Social Work, National Child Welfare Training Center.

Green, James W. (1995). *Cultural awareness in the human services*. (2nd ed.) Boston: Allyn & Bacon.

Green, James W., & Leigh, James W. (1989). Teaching ethnographic methods to social service workers. *Practicing Anthropology, 11*(3), 8–10.

Greenbaum, Lenora, & Holmes, Ivory H. (1983). The use of folktales in social work practice. *Social Casework, 54*(7), 414–418.

Guberman, Karen. (1992, Spring). Social work and the new diversity: How social work is responding to our changing society. *SSA Magazine*, 2–5.

Hamilton, Gordon. (1967). *Theory and practice of social case work* (2nd ed.). New York: Columbia University Press.

Hammersley, Martyn. (1990). *Ethnographic research: A critical guide*. New York: Longman.

Harvey, Aminifu. (1995). The issue of skin color in psychotherapy with African Americans. *Families in Society, 76*(1), 3–10.

Henson, James. (1983). *Cultural perspectives in family therapy*. Rockville, MD: Aspen Systems Corporation.

Hine, Darlene Clark. (1994). Rape and the inner lives of black women in the Middle West: Preliminary thoughts on the culture of dissemblance. In Ellen Carol DuBois & Vicki L. Ruiz (Eds.), *Unequal sisters: A multi-cultural reader in U.S. women's history* (pp. 292–298). New York: Routledge.

Ho, Man Keung. (1982). Case studies. *Practice Digest, 5*(3), 6–7.

Hollis, Florence, & Wood, Mary. (1981). *Casework: A psychosocial therapy*. (3rd ed.). New York: McGraw-Hill.

Hooks, Bell. (1994). *Teaching to transgress*. New York: Routledge.

Howard, Harold P. (1971). *Sacajawea*. Norman, OK: University of Oklahoma Press.

Johnson, Louise A. (1986). *Social work practice*. Boston: Allyn & Bacon.

Jourard, Sidney M., & Jaffee, Peggy E. (1970). Influence of an interviewer's self-disclosure on the self-disclosing behavior of interviewees. *Journal of Consulting Psychology, 17*(3), 252–257.

Kadushin, Alfred. (1972). *The social work interview*. New York: Columbia University Press.

Kagle, Jill Doner. (1988). Overcoming "person-al" errors in assessment. *ARETE, 13*(2), 35–40.

Kapuscinski, Ryzard. (1988). America as a collage. *New Perspectives Quarterly, 5*(2), 39–46.

Kaufman, Sharon. (1986). *The ageless self*. New York: New American Library.

Kenmore, T. K. (1987). Negotiating with clients: A study of clinical practice experience. *Social Service Review, 61*(1), 132–143.

King, Joseph. (1995). *Narratives of possibility: Social movements, collective stories and the dilemmas of practice*. Paper presented at the New Social Movement and Community Organizing Conference, School of Social Work, University of Washington.

Kleinman, Arthur. (1988, a). *The illness narratives: Suffering, healing and the human condition*. New York: Basic Books.

Kleinman, Arthur. (1988, b). *Rethinking psychiatry: From cultural category to personal experience*. New York: The Free Press.

Kleinman, Arthur, Eisenberg, Leon, & Good, Byron. (1978). Culture, illness and care: Clinical lessons from anthropologic and cross-cultural research. *Annals of Internal Medicine, 88*(2), 251–258.

Kracke, Ward H. (1987). A psychoanalyst in the field: Erickson's contribution to anthropology. In Jerome Rabow, Gerald M. Platt, & Marion Goldman (Eds.), *Advances in psychoanalytic sociology*. Malabar, FL: Robert E. Krieger.

Krajewski-Jaime, Elvia R., Brown, Kaaren Strauch, Ziefert, Marjorie, & Kaufman, Elizabeth. (1996). Utilizing international clinical practice to build inter-cultural sensitivity in social work students. *Journal of Multicultural Social Work, 4* (2), 15–29.

Kumabe, Kazuye T., Nishida, Chikae, & Hepworth, Dean H. (1985). *Bridging ethnocultural diversity in social work and health*. Honolulu, HI: University of Hawaii School of Social Work.

LaFromboise, Teresa D., & Dixon, David N. (1981). American Indian perceptions of trustworthiness in a counseling interview. *Journal of Counseling Psychology, 28*(2), 135–139.

Lantz, Jim, & Pegram, Mary. (1989). Cross cultural curative factors and clinical social work. *Journal of Independent Social Work, 4*(1), 55–68.

Leigh, James W. (1985). The ethnically competent social worker. In Joan Laird and Ann Hartman (Eds.), *A handbook of child welfare* (pp. 449–459). New York: The Free Press.

Levin, Jerome David. (1993). *Slings and arrows: Narcissistic injury and its treatment.* Northvale, NJ: Jason Aronson.

Levine, Elaine, & Padilla, Amado. (1980). *Crossing cultures in therapy: Pluristic counseling for Hispanics.* Monterey, CA: Brooks/Cole.

Levinson, Daniel, Merrifield, John, & Berg, Kenneth. (1967). Becoming a patient. *Archives of General Psychiatry, 17,* 385–406.

Lewis, Harold. (1982). *The intellectual base for social work practice.* New York: The Haworth Press.

Lewis, Ronald. (1985). Cultural perspectives on treatment modalities with Native Americans. In Martin Bloom (Ed.), *Life span development* (2nd. ed.) (pp. 458–464). New York: Macmillan.

Lewis, Thomas. (1974). An Indian healer's preventative medicine procedures. *Hospital and Community Psychiatry, 25*(2), 94–95.

Lincoln, Yvonna S., & Guba, Ergon. (1985). *Naturalistic inquiry.* Beverly Hills, CA: Sage.

Lindsay, Isabel Burns. (1947). Race as a factor in the caseworker's role. *Journal of Social Casework, 28*(3), 101–107.

Lockhart, Barbetta. (1981). Historic distrust and the counseling of American Indians and Alaskan natives. *White Cloud Journal, 2*(3), 31–34.

Logan, Sadye. (1985). Review of *Color in a white society. Social Work, 30*(4), 376.

Lum, Doman. (1986). *Social work practice and people of color.* Monterey, CA: Brooks/Cole.

MacIntyre, Alastair. (1988). *How to be a North American.* Washington, DC: Federation of State Humanities Councils.

Maluccio, Anthony N., & Marlow, Wilma D. (1974). The case for contract. *Social Work, 19*(1), 28–36.

Maple, Frank F. (1985). *Dynamic interviewing: An introduction to counseling.* Beverly Hills, CA: Sage.

Marziali, Elsa. (1988). The first session: An interpersonal encounter. *Social Casework, 6*(1), 23–27.

McAdoo, Harriet. (1982). Demographic trends for people of color. *Social Work, 27*(1), 15–23.

McPhatter, Anna R. (1997). Cultural competence in child welfare. What is it? How do we achieve it? What happens without it?. *Child Welfare. LXXVI*(1), 255–278.

Mead, Margaret. (1972). *Blackberry winter: My earlier years.* New York: William Morrow.

Mead, Margaret, & Calas, Nicholas. (1953). *Primitive heritage.* New York: Random House.

Mercer, Susan. (1996). Navajo elderly people in a reservation nursing home: Admission predictors and culture care practice. *Social Work, 41*(2), 181–189.

Meyer, Carel. (1985). The institutional context of child welfare. In Joan Laird and Ann Hartman (Eds.), *A Handbook of child welfare* (pp. 10–115). New York: The Free Press.

Melton, Lucy Ann. (1980). Introduction. In John Langston Gwaltney, *Drylongso: A portrait of black America* (pp. xxiv). New York: Random House.

Miranda, Manuel R., & Kitano, Harry H. L. (Eds.). *Mental health research and practice in minority communities: Development of culturally sensitive training programs.* Rockville, MD: National Institute of Mental Health.

Mitchell, Jacqueline. (1982). Reflections of a black social scientist: Some struggles, some hopes. *Harvard Educational Review, 52*(1), 27–44.

Moore, Robert B. (1992). Racist stereotyping in the English language. In Margaret L. Anderson & Patricia Hill Collins (Eds.), *Race, class, and gender* (pp. 317–329). Belmont, CA: Wadsworth.

Murray, Albert. (1970). *The ommni-Americans: New perspectives on black experience and American culture.* New York: Outerbridge and Dienstfrey.

Norton, Dolores G. (1993). Diversity, early socialization, and temporal development: The dual perspective revisited. *Social Work, 38*(1), 82–90.

Norton, Dolores G., Brown, Eddie F., Brown, Edwin G., Francis, E. Aracelis, Mirase, Kenji, & Valle, Ramon. (1978). *The dual perspective: Inclusion of ethnic minority content in social work education.* New York: Council on Social Work Education.

Perlman, Helen Harris. (1972). *Relationship: The heart of helping people.* Chicago: University of Chicago Press.

———. (1957). *Social casework: A problem solving process.* Chicago: University of Chicago Press.

Ramsell, Penny Smith, & Ramsell, Earle R. (1994). Counselor and client perceptions of the effect of social and physical contact on the therapeutic process. *Clinical Social Work Journal, 22*(1), 91–104.

Reed, Ishmeal. (1988). *Writin' is fightin'.* New York: Atheneum.

Rodwell, Mary K. (1987). Naturalistic inquiry: An alternative model for social assessment. *Social Service Review, 61*(2), 231–246.

Rojek, Chris, & Collins, Stewart A. (1987). Contract or con trick. *British Journal of Social Work, 17*(2), 199–211.

Rorty, Richard. (1989). *Contingency, irony and solidarity.* New York: Cambridge University Press.

Rothman, Jack, Gant, Larry M., & Hnat, Stephen A. (1985, June). Mexican American family structure. *Social Service Review, 59*(2), 197–215.

Saaleby, Dennis. (1994). Culture, theory and narrative: The intersection of meaning in social work. *Social Work, 39*(4), 351–359.

Saari, Carolyn. (1991). *The creation of meaning in social work.* New York: The Guilford Press.

Sabin, Edwin L. (1917). *Opening the west with Lewis and Clark.* Philadelphia: Lippincott.

Sampson, Edward. (1993). *Celebrating the other: A dialogic account of human nature.* Boulder, CO: Westview Press.

Saunders, Lyle. (1954). *Cultural differences and medical care.* New York: Russell Sage Foundation.

Schuetz, Alfred. (1960). The stranger: An essay in social psychology. In Maurice R. Stein, Arthur J. Vidich, & David Manning White (Eds.), *Identity and Anxiety* (pp. 98–109). Glencoe, IL: The Free Press.

Seabury, Brett. (1979). Negotiating sound contracts with clients. *Public Welfare, 37*(2), 33–38.

———. (1985). The beginning phrase: Engagement, initial assessment and contracting. In Joan Laird and Ann Hartman (Eds.), *A Handbook of Child Welfare* (pp. 355–359). New York: The Free Press.

See, Lethia A. (1986). *Tensions and tangles between Afro-Americans and southeast Asian refugees: A study of the conflict.* Atlanta, GA: Wright.

Shoemaker, Nancy. (1995, Summer). Native American women in history. *OAH Magazine of History,* 10–14.

Shriver, Joe M. (1995). *Human behavior and the social environment.* Boston: Allyn & Bacon.

Shulman, Lawrence. (1979). *The skills of helping.* Itasca, IL: F. E. Peacock.

Shweder, Richard A. (1986, September 21). Storytelling among the anthropologists. *The New York Times Book Review 9*(7), 38–39.

Silva, Juliette. (1983). Cross-cultural and cross-ethnic assessment. In Guadalupe Gibson (Ed.), *Our kingdom stands on brittle glass* (pp. 59–66). Washington, DC: National Association of Social Workers.

Simmel, George. (1980). The stranger. In Kurt Wolfe (Ed.), *The sociology of George Simmel* (pp. 402–409). Glencoe, IL: The Free Press.

Slonim, Maureen. (1991). *Children, culture, and ethnicity.* New York: Garland.

Solomon, Barbara. (1976). *Black empowerment: Social work in oppressed communities.* New York: Columbia University Press.

———. (1985). Assessment, service and black families. In Sylvia Simms Gray, Ann Hartman, & Ellen S. Saalberg (Eds.), *Empowering the black family* (pp. 10–20). Ann Arbor, MI: National Child Welfare Training Center, University of Michigan School of Social Work.

———. (1985). The roundtable. In Sylvia Simms Gray, Ann Hartman, & Ellen S. Saalberg (Eds.), *Empowering the black family* (p. 73). Ann Arbor, MI: National Child Welfare Training Center, University of Michigan School of Social Work.

Spradley, James P. (1979). *The ethnographic interview.* New York: Holt, Rinehart & Winston.

Steinberg, Stephen. (1981). *The ethnic myth: Race, ethnicity, and class in America.* New York: Atheneum.

Sue, Stanley, & Zane, Nolan. (1987). The role of culture and cultural techniques in psychotherapy: A critique and reformation. *American Psychologist, 42*(1), 37–45.

Szasz, Thomas S. (1971). The sane slave. *American Journal of Psychotherapy, 25*(3), 226–239.

Talbert, Wynn, & Sullivan, Peggy (1988). *Competency based child welfare practice: Research findings.* Fresno, CA: Child Welfare Training Project, California State University, Fresno, School of Health and Social Work.

Thornton, Serene, & Garrett, Kendra J. (1995). Ethnography as a bridge to multicultural practice. *Journal of Social Work Education. 31*(6), 67–74.

Thurman, Howard. (1965). *The luminous darkness.* New York: Harper and Row.

Time. (1985, July 8). Immigration: The changing face of America, 26–32.

Tropp, Emanuel. (1974). Three problematic concepts: Clients, help and worker. *Social Casework, 55*(1), 19–35.

Tumin, Melvin M., & Plotch, Walter. (1977). *Pluralism in a democratic society.* New York: Praeger.

U.S. News and World Report. (1996, March 25). Ahead: A very different nation, 16.

Vontress, Clemmont E. (1971). Racial differences: Impediments to rapport. *Journal of Counseling Psychology, 18*(1), 7–13.

Watson, Lawrence C., & Watson-Franke, Maria-Barbara. (1985). *Interpreting life histories: An anthropological inquiry.* New Brunswick, NJ: Rutgers University Press.

Werner, Oswald, & Schoepfle, G. Mark. (1987). *Systematic fieldwork: Foundations of ethnography and interviewing.* Beverly Hills, CA: Sage.

Whittaker, James K., & Tracy, Elizabeth M. (1989). *Social treatment.* New York: Aldine DeGruyter.

Wick, Robert J. (1977). *Strategies and intervention techniques for the human services.* Philadelphia: Lippincott.

Williams, Leon F. (1988). Framework for introducing racial and ethnic content into the curriculum. In Carolyn Jacobs and Dorcas D. Bowles (Eds.), *Ethnicity and race: critical concepts in social work* (pp. 167–184). Silver Springs, MD: National Association of Social Workers.

Wilson, Linda. (1982). *The skills of ethnic competence.* Unpublished resource paper. Seattle: University of Washington School of Social Work.

Young-Bruehl, Elisabeth. (1996). *The anatomy of prejudices.* Cambridge, MA: Harvard University Press.

INDEX